LETTERS FROM EVEREST

LETTERS FROM EVEREST

Unpublished Letters from Mallory's Life and Death in the Mountains

GEORGE MALLORY

&

TOM NEWTON DUNN

**WILLIAM
COLLINS**

William Collins
An imprint of HarperCollins*Publishers*
1 London Bridge Street
London SE1 9GF

WilliamCollinsBooks.com

HarperCollins*Publishers*
Macken House
39/40 Mayor Street Upper
Dublin 1
D01 C9W8, Ireland

First published in Great Britain in 2024 by William Collins

1

A catalogue record for this book is available from the British Library

ISBN 978-0-00-870287-8 (hardback)
ISBN 978-0-00-870288-5 (trade paperback)

Typeset in Minion Pro by Jouve (UK), Milton Keynes

Printed and bound in Great Britain by CPI Group (UK) Ltd, Croydon

MIX
Paper | Supporting
responsible forestry
FSC™ C007454
FSC
www.fsc.org

This book contains FSC™ certified paper and other controlled
sources to ensure responsible forest management.

For more information visit: www.harpercollins.co.uk/green

To my extraordinary great-uncle and also his children, who picked up his burden when he had gone

CONTENTS

CONTENTS

INTRODUCTION: 'YOUR LOVING SON GEORGE'

'Why do you want to climb Mount Everest, Mr Mallory?' It was a question George was repeatedly asked, wherever he went. One day, in March 1923, he offered up a wistful response that swiftly entered into folklore. 'Because it's there.' The remark, to a *New York Times* journalist when George was on a lecture tour of the United States, has been quoted ever since as an inspiring example of man's indomitable spirit of determination to overcome any challenge.

But was it that? George's elder sister Mary had an alternative explanation. Her passionate younger brother's impatience with people who didn't share his dreams was well known among his three siblings. The remark, Mary (my great-grandmother) liked to say, was actually a quick-witted put down for 'another silly American, asking the same silly question'.

George Mallory had multiple personas that often contradicted each other. Mountaineer, explorer, teacher, dreamer, revolutionary, husband, father, bisexual, Bloomsbury pin-up, Army officer, author, hero, failure. He was all of those, often at the same time – a true polymath, now remembered as one of the early 20th century's most extraordinary Englishmen.

Some of these personas are well documented, others remain private if they are remembered at all. Yet none of them have defined George more than his tragic death.

He and climbing partner Andrew 'Sandy' Irvine were last seen alive through binoculars as two moving dots, at 12.50pm on June 8th, 1924, just 800 feet short of Everest's summit. They were 'going strong for the top', according to their fellow expedition member who spotted them before they were enveloped by cloud. They never came down, and Mallory and Irvine's disappearance sparked mountaineering's greatest and most romantic mystery.

What exactly happened to them, and did they make it to the top before they died? Were they actually the first to ascend the planet's highest peak, some 29 years before the official record holders, Edmund Hillary and Tenzing Norgay?

The discovery of George's broken but well-preserved body not far below Everest's summit in 1999 added more clues, but none of them definitive. Irvine was believed to have been climbing with the pair's Kodak camera, and his body has never been found, so the mystery still endures 100 years on.

The odds were against them, and they knew it. The rest of their climbing party were exhausted and no longer fit, and a storm from the arriving monsoon was rapidly closing in. By today's standards, they were also appallingly ill-equipped, climbing with only the most rudimentary oxygen equipment – designed by Irvine, a 22-year-old Oxford student, himself.

So why did Mallory and Irvine press on? Press on, ever higher towards Everest's summit, where the temperature never rises above -20°C and winds of more than 100mph can push the wind-chill temperature down to as low as -83°C. Was it courage or stupidity? Recklessness or bad luck? Narcissism or heroism?

Much has been written about Mallory the myth. The schoolboy superhero, full of derring-do. The Bloomsbury aesthete, with whom men and women fell in love and he loved in equal measure. But who was George the human being, the real person? That side of him is far less known, but it can be tantalisingly glimpsed in the large and previously unseen tranche of letters that George wrote to his mother, which are published here in full for the first time.

These letters span a lifetime, the significant majority of George's 37 years, from his early school days at Winchester, right the way through to his last ever letter home, from Everest's Camp I, 10 days before he disappeared. And they reveal so much of his character, which they chart throughout his life. Whether battling Eton on the cricket pitch or Everest's notorious Second Step, George's key character traits remained constant: passionate, charming, driven, restless, impatient. They are the traits that won him worldwide notoriety and the traits that killed him.

Before the letters were stored away for safekeeping in an old family trunk decades ago, George's mother Annie had diligently catalogued them into the various chapters of his life: school at Winchester, university at Cambridge, Charterhouse where he taught, the Western Front where he fought, and from the three different expeditions to Everest in the early 1920s. Generally respected as the best climber in the country at the time, George was the only one of the 26 total members of the expeditions to go on all three; 1921, 1922 and 1924.

The letters are also startlingly confessional. A son's relationship with his mother is like no other: intimate, proud, trusting. Who else can you share your greatest fears with and make your biggest boasts to, without fear of judgement or betrayal? Mothers adore their sons, no matter what. George bared his true soul to his.

George and Annie were very alike. Born Annie Jebb, she had revolt in her genes. She was descended from not one but two reforming Whig prime ministers of the 19th century, Earl Grey and Lord John Russell. Unlike George's father – the dependable parish rector, the Reverend Herbert Leigh-Mallory – Annie was also a romantic and a dreamer. She was physically beautiful, emotionally highly strung and domestically chaotic. The pair were close, and George's letters reveal a deep respect and love for her.

Also constant throughout the letters are two more things. First, George's lifelong love affair with the mountains, from his schoolboy trips to the Alps to his dream of conquering Everest. The dream became an obsession, and at times a frightening one. George is always honest about just how daunting a challenge it was, writing halfway through the 1921 expedition: 'Every day when I see Everest I am rather appalled. It is a terrifyingly formidable mountain, the faces are appallingly steep. Sometimes it seems an impossible idea that anyone should ever reach the summit.'

George was a keen photographer, and took his own pictures during the expeditions – some of which are published here too. His letters and pictures reinforce again just how amateur the first attempts on Everest were, and how eccentric those were who made them. As gentlemen, they famously climbed in tweed, Norfolk jackets, woolly jumpers and silk underwear. They puffed on pipes, read Shakespeare to each other inside their shivering tents and insisted on taking four cases of champagne with them over the Tibetan plains and up the Rongbuk Glacier.

At lower levels when it was hot, they trekked naked. One photograph captures George wearing only a daysack, a trilby and a broad grin. At higher levels, their only specialist equipment was what they could cobble together themselves. George's big sister Mary enjoyed telling her grandchildren how she knitted him especially thick socks for his trips. Before one expedition, she also watched him hammer nails through the soles of his walking boots to give himself more grip on Everest's snow and ice.

The second constant through the letters is George's never-ending search for meaning and purpose in a very troubled and at times bleak world. It's impossible to really understand what was in the minds of the pioneer Everest explorers, the hopes and fears that drove them on, without appreciating what so many of them had just gone through on the Western Front. The slaughter and devastation, the pointlessness of it all, had a searing effect on their whole generation. When they did emerge from the trenches alive, they were determined to make something positive out of the world. To do something with their lives – lives that many of them didn't think they would still have by the war's end.

George was no exception. In his first letter home from France after Armistice Day, he writes of having 'escaped so many chances of death, it is surprising to find myself a survivor'. He asks: 'We can never thank God enough, and can we ever live nobly enough to be worth of such a gift?'

Climbing mountains, and a meaning to life – for George, Mount Everest fused the two together, and eventually they became one. Summitting Everest became his purpose for existing.

Some of George's letters are long, some short. Some lavishly discursive, others economically factual – much depending on how much time he had to write them, and the mood he was in. Juxtaposed with the profound is the mundanity of early 20th-century existence; wonderfully bitchy moans about his tedious dining companions, delight at the successful decoration of a new home and more than one adolescent plea for money to help him fund his latest climbing trip. All shed light on a fascinating life lived during a tumultuous period in history.

Some are written on Alpine hotel stationery with resplendent mastheads, or the grand colonial dark blue note paper of 'Government House, Darjeeling'; others from his long passages to and from India, onboard the steamers SS *Sardinia* or the SS *California*.

On Everest, he paints meticulous descriptions of the awesome peaks around him, seen up close for the first time by any man, and the stunning pinks and oranges of a Himalayan dawn. He also details the extraordinarily challenging conditions that were an ever-present battle for the expeditions.

In one letter home from inside a chilly tent at Base Camp a month before he died, George's ink begins to run thin and dry, and in the next sentence he switches to pencil, with the simple explanatory note in parentheses '(sorry the ink has begun to freeze)'.

Included too are a few letters that George wrote to his sister Mary, who he was also very close to. There is also one from his father, Reverend Herbert, to his mother Annie that reveals an un-biblical thought on why he was so surprised George was to marry. Finally, there are four letters from George's widow Ruth. Written in the immediate months after his death, they reveal the terrible rawness of her pain and the desolation of her loss. Even today, they are unbearably sad to read.

George's life ended prematurely aged 37, and in tragedy. But his life wasn't tragic. Throughout his letters, two emotions also recur time and again, from school and university to his philosophising, fighting, falling in love and Everest: hope and ambition. Perhaps the two most human emotions of all.

Whether he was on the receiving end of poetry or a witty put-down, the dogged *New York Times* journalist back in early 1923 was not to be deterred. He asked George to expand on what he meant by 'because it's there' as a reason for conquering Everest. George obliged, and their full exchange is also quoted in the ensuing article (which was headlined 'Climbing Mount Everest is work for Supermen'). Surely you're climbing to obtain valuable scientific findings, the American suggested.

'Yes, the expeditions make geological surveys, and collect specimens both geological and botanical,' George replied. 'They are very valuable. But do you think Shackleton went to the South Pole to make scientific observations? He used the observations he did make to help finance the next trip. Sometimes science is the excuse for the exploration. I think it is rarely the reason. Everest is the highest mountain in the world, and no man has reached its summit. Its existence is a challenge. The answer is instinctive – a part, I suppose, of man's desire to conquer the universe.'

1

WINCHESTER, CAMBRIDGE AND THE ALPS (1900–1909)

George's first climb was to the roof of his village church. An impressive feat, as he was only seven years old at the time.

George Herbert Leigh-Mallory was born on June 18th, 1886, in Mobberley, a prosperous and pretty village in Cheshire. The church he scaled was his father's, the Reverend Herbert Leigh-Mallory, who was the rector of the parish. The job was hereditary, as it had been in the gift of the Mallory family for centuries.

George was the second of four children, preceded by elder sister Mary, and followed by younger sister Avie and finally younger brother Trafford. Herbert, his wife Annie and the children lived in a big manor house close to the church with a plentiful supply of servants. Yet they were often in financial difficulties, because Herbert and Annie were hopeless with money. They spent wildly, always having the latest gadgets (the newly invented vacuum cleaner or an ice cream maker) and never serving the same joint of meat twice as leftovers.

Emotional and highly strung, Annie struggled to hold on to her servants, not least because of her habit of ringing every bell at once to summon them all at the same time. She also regularly clashed with the children's governess. 'Why is it that every time Mother comes into the play-room, a row starts?' Mary remembered George once asking. Mild-mannered Herbert seldom intervened, so the children grew up unruly and spirited, and with a sense of adventure that Annie insisted on instilling in them. For George, that often meant climbing. His sisters remember George climbing anything and everything, and often chal-lenging them to dare him. He had a lithe build, but was strong and a natural athlete, as well as bright.

Aged eight, George was sent away to board at Glengorse prep school on the south coast, before winning a maths scholarship to Winchester College, where he was also the school's best gymnast. His letters to his mother from school bubble with enthusiasm for his 'simply ripping' outdoor adventures and sporting endeavours. An over-whelming need to beat Eton in the two rival schools' annual cricket clashes – in which George played – constantly appears.

It was while a student at Winchester College that George first discovered the mountains. Graham Irving, an accom-plished mountaineer and a member of the Alpine Club, was a master there and was told of George's adventurous spirit. Irving recruited him for a summer trip to the Alps. George had to beg his cash-strapped parents to fork out for his rail ticket, but as soon as he got there, he was mesmerised.

In a letter home from Switzerland, George told his mother it had been 'inexplicably glorious to see peak after peak touched with the pink glow of its first sun, which slowly spread until the whole top was a flaming fire'.

There were also climbing trips from Mobberley to Snowdonia with brother Trafford, making the 80-mile trip on bicycles with their ropes over their shoulders. The brothers enjoyed one such trip so much, they announced they would be staying in their hay barn lodgings 'indefinitely'. In a joint letter to their mother, they also thanked her for sending silver spoons but told her it would be 'very pleasant' if she could instead send them a homemade cake.

George won another scholarship, to read history at Magdalene College, Cambridge (where Mallory Court is now named after him). At university, he also rowed, captaining his college's triumphant eight boat. At Cambridge George also began to move in aesthetic circles, as his more flamboyant handwriting and the thick artists' sketching paper that he wrote home on gives away. A close friend that he made at Cambridge and also climbed with was Geoffrey Keynes, the younger brother of the renowned economist Maynard Keynes. The First World War poet Rupert Brooke was also a friend, along with other fledgling luminaries of the Bloomsbury set, which spawned from Cambridge in the early 1900s.

George's university days were regularly punctuated by climbing parties to Wales, as well as to France and

Switzerland – a treat he relished: 'To see the Alps again! How glorious it will be, after dreaming of them.' George developed a unique climbing style that was beguiling to watch, as fast as it was graceful. Neither was he put off by two incidents that he reported back to his mother: 'a horrible accident to two Swiss men on the Jungfrau, a most grisly affair', and a master at Eton 'killed climbing alone'. Fear does not seem to have been a word in his adolescent vocabulary.

The College
Winchester
September 22, 1900

My dear Mother,

I'm sorry I didn't write to you before. I came here all right
on Wednesday, alright, although by the 4 o'clock train
instead of the 5.10, as otherwise I should have to have
waited an hour at Waterloo which I didn't exactly relish.
I found Mr Rendall, who took me up to the warden, who
admitted me to college, and afterwards gave me tea.

I had a ripping time down at Sydenham; we went to the
Crystal Palace, the Zoo & Hippodrome, all of which
I enjoyed very much.

I like being here very much – ever so much better than
Glengorse, & I like the men better too (instead of chaps we
always say men): we have plenty of work to do, and I'm
afraid I'm running you up a heavy book bill; we shan't
begin playing footer – the Winchester game – for some
time yet; we get up at 6.15, and begin work – morning lines
it's called at 7.00.

With much love,
Ever your loving son,
George.

The College
Winchester
October 14, 1900

My dear Mother,

I am awfully glad you're coming down on Thursday, I
suppose you'll be staying a night with the Grahams, and I
have ventured to hope that Avie will come too, as she is
going away sometime then.

It's simply lovely being here; 'life is like a dream', I enjoy it
immensely. I hope I shall be able to tell you everything we
do, and that you'll be able to see everything here on
Thursday.

I am glad father has come back well from Scotland; he
must write and tell me how his choir feud is
getting on.

I spend most of my afternoon time reading in our
library – Moberly library – which is an absolute
nightmare: however, it's not worth while my telling
you all this now when you're coming down so
shortly.

You must write to me again before Thursday and let me
know all you propose to do, which I have no doubt
involves a great deal. When you come down you may as

well bring my chessmen, if they're not on request at
Hobcroft.

With love to all at home,
I remain,
Yr. loving son George

P.S. Please tell Trafford from me that he must back up and
become a mathematician, and if he can't read decently by
next hols I shall kick him.

The College
Winchester
June 30, 1901

My dear Mother,

I had a simply glorious time on Friday and Saturday; on Friday I rode to Godalming, which is 25 miles from here; on the way there, there was a hill $4\frac{1}{2}$ miles long, between Alresford and Alton and a corresponding down hill of $3\frac{1}{2}$ miles long on the other side. Coming back was simply glorious; cousin Polly rode with me as far as Farnham, which is 25 miles from here, and after that I rode at the average rate of 15 miles an hour, getting here shortly under $1\frac{3}{4}$ hrs. Yesterday I spent a simply ripping day at Eton: on the first innings, which was played on Friday we gained 26 runs, the scores being 259 and 233 runs, going in again on Saturday, we made only 186, and left them plenty of time to make the runs; they then went in and made about 79 for 4 wickets, and afterwards 180 for 8; the match then began to get frightfully exciting but unfortunately they eventually knocked off the runs without the loss of another wicket: We were at a great disadvantage in being without the service of McDonell, our captain, and who was also captain last year and did very well in that match; he had got a very hard ball on the head in Lord's practice, which gave him a slight concussion.

Please thank father very much for the tin he sent me, which was <u>wholly</u> adequate, and also Aunt Emma. Father wanted to know on which Sunday we had the Holy Communion; most Sundays it will be administered.

With best love to all,
I remain,
Yr. loving son,
George

P.S. Elections begin on July 9, and very likely those will be some candidates from Glengorse.

The College
Winchester
July 3, 1904

My dear Mother,

My last letter of Friday evening forgot its most important object. I meant to send you the photo I have had taken here; I think it is very good on the whole: your birthday present is a most excellent one & I am very pleased at being able to give my photo to a lot of people here who wanted one.

I am quite aware that cash is very scarce just now, which makes my expedition to Switzerland seem rather a nuisance. The only expense will be the ticket out there, I don't know how much that will come to, but I hope Gra will give me something towards that – by way of a birthday present – ; then to the cost of keeping me at home for the three weeks or whatever it is that I am in Switzerland would amount to something considerable, so that if you reckon the cost of the expedition from that point of view it will come to something very small, I fancy. The worst of my exam comes on this week and I am not anticipating any great joy there.

I suppose Mary has returned home by now; it was rather a pity she was not able to stay longer on the second day of Eton match.

With much love,
Yr. loving son,
George

P.S. I am sending two different photos; I daresay Father or
Mary might like one.

August 6, 1904
Hotel Napoleon
Bourg St Pierre

My dear Mother,

We have had an awfully jolly time at our first staying place Bourg St Pierre. Arrived here on Thursday evening, driving from Martigny & seen the most lovely views of sunset. Yesterday morning at 2 a.m. we got up, had some coffee & after an hour's uphill drive arrived at the centre at the bottom of the Vélan at about 6000 ft.

The first few hundred feet of the climb was in moonlight – the town afterwards was glorious. We breakfasted after ascending steep grass slopes for over 3000 ft – an awful sweat: I didn't feel actually tired, but had no inclination to eat; the sun had risen on Mont Blanc which was a perfectly delightful pink & we watched it spread across a range of huge peaks with infinite delight. After breakfast we had a short descent from a point of vantage & then crossed over a moraine & ascended another small glacier with one or two crevasses, then came to a perfectly ripping little bergschrund which we crossed to a narrow snow bridge about 20 yds along; above it was a steep slope of hard snow which was easily ascended with the help of an ice axe. We then took off the ropes & got onto some easy rocks which we ascended for about 1000 ft. to the W arête of this mountain; the latter was a sharp ridge, which one could first walk along with a drop of a few hundred feet on both sides. I was already beginning to feel mountain sick, but we went on & after another 300 ft or so was actually sick. After going up about 100 ft from the arête we had a rather prolonged halt, & were taken by a storm. I was again sick and though we were only 600 ft from the top, & could have got there in $3/4$ hr at most as we should have had no view & I naturally wasn't much enjoying it; we decided to descend.

I was sick more times on the way down & didn't feel well again until we were walking below the moraine. However, we had had some magnificent views & I enjoyed the remainder of the day immensely. We are just starting for the Ballé hut (9000 ft) & are going to ascend the Grand Combin from there to-morrow. Although we only got to 11,600 ft up on Friday, having been here two days since will make a tremendous lot of differences & I hope to evade mountain sickness, even when over 14,000 ft high.

I didn't feel the least bit tired last night, although getting down grass slopes as steep as the ones we were on yesterday is almost as tiring as anything; so as far as muscular power goes I feel very well satisfied. We have already seen $1/2$ a dozen waterfalls infinitely better than any in England; there is one only about 200 yards from us here in which a big volume of water descends for about 150 ft, then 250 ft about 20 yds further on. On either side are the most beautiful cliffs & trees. I managed to get just above the

first one within a few feet of the place where it leans over;
the rainbow effect of the sun on the slopes was ripping.

No more now as we are just going to start.

Much love to all,
Yr. loving son,
George

Enclose photos for Mary, which I meant to send before.

August 22, 1906
Grand Hôtel
Arolla Hotel du Mont Collon

My dear Mother,

Thanks very much for your letter wh. I was very glad to get; I had one from father also yesterday; he seems to be enjoying a little rest. We have had rather bad luck with weather, the plans last week being quite spoilt, but still have managed to do something. On Monday we did Mont Collon, taking Miss Irving, which made it quite a long expedition. Tuesday we had intended to do the Dent Perroc wh. is quite a good day, but took a well-earned sled instead. Tuesday night, Wednesday & Thursday were wet, but on Friday morning we started in doubtful weather for Mont Pleureur; the weather cleared beautifully & we had an awfully jolly day of $13^{1}/_{2}$ hrs traversing the mountain; on Saturday we come back here over Mont Blanc de Cheilon which was most enjoyable & took under 12 hrs getting back here at 4.30 for tea. We went to church on Sunday morning & up to the Bertol but in the afternoon getting there in under 4 hrs shortly before 7 o'clock. We had about the most beautiful sunset I have ever seen: on the east a huge snow field separates the Col de Bertol from the Dent Blanche, the Matterhorn and the Dent D'Herens and in the west the sun was setting behind many smaller mountains across the Arolla valley & the effects of shadow & clouds were simply marvellous. At 3.15 yesterday morning we started by moonlight across the huge snow field on the most delightful hard crisp snow & after the most enjoyable walk & a short scramble over easy rocks we found ourselves on the arête of the Dent Blanche at 7.15. The sun of course had risen as we neared the Dent Blanche & as we had already gone up quite a lot the view was splendid right over to the Mont Blanc range; it was altogether too inexpressibly glorious to see peak after peak touched with the pink glow of its first sun, which slowly spread until the whole top was a flaming fire, & that against a sky with varied tints of leaden blue. We had a halt & breakfast for nearly an hour on the arête & then climbed straight to the top in a little over 3 hrs, arriving there at 10.25; there was lots of good climbing to be done & I can quite understand what an awful mountain it must be in bad conditions. Yesterday we had excellent conditions & our time was quite good I think: we had no difficulty coming down, but a most laborious walk across the snow field; the rest of the party were waiting with tea for us at the Bertol hut as pre-arranged & rejoiced with due rejoicing; the Dent Blanche was the one peak we had set out hearts upon doing; Guy Bullock goes back to England to-morrow, of course there were only we three in the party, which by the by was the only one on the mountain.

I think it very unlikely that you will see me before Sept 2: we hope to end up with a few valleys & passes which will take about 4 days.

The rest of the party consist of Mrs Tyndale & 2 Misses Tyndales who are all very nice & most solicitous for our welfare even when son Harry is not with us; there is also Leach who has left Winchester a year [ago] & is a most excellent man.

Eddy Morgan said that he would probably have to leave us on Thursday following Sept 2, but I have asked him if possible to stay till Monday following: I suppose the most convenient arrangement for me to sleep in Trafford's room & that gentleman to sleep out, if he is at home then.

Much love to all,
Yr. loving son,
George

Xmas
1906
Wishes

May Christmas shed the Afterglow
Of Summers passed away
On the glad Hills that watched the Dawn
Of Everlasting Day

G.H.L.M.

Cows leigh
Capel Curig
Sunday
10 August 1908

[Trafford writes:]
My dear Mother,

We are having a glorious time here. We went up Tryfan (the central buttress) yesterday & an excellent climb. Thank you for sending the silver spoons & forks.

We are very comfortable now. We are in a kind of hut, which has a cow stall at one end, which is used for cows only during the winter; all the other part is used for hay. It is situated just beside a stream, in which there is the most glorious bathing among the rocks, there being one place in which one can sit & it is as smooth & comfortable to sit in as a bath & the water comes up to the middle of one's chest. It is so absolutely glorious here that I cannot find words to express it, so George is going to have a turn at the pencil.

[George writes:]
Trafford really wants to have what he calls a 'bed rehearsal'. And on what beds! Some [illegible] hay covered with blankets – no mattresses can beat that. If Mary & Avie will come (we intend to stay indefinitely) we can partition the hut. Or we could probably find rooms for them in some farm house near by; there is a small cottage not far off which I think we ought to take en famille next year.

It's not properly raining yet & I'm afraid it will be wet
to-morrow. We have had a peaceful Sunday – & rather a
pious one beginning with an 8 a.m. service.

When you send the shirts, we should like a second tin mug
($4^{1}/_{2}$d) which we can't procure here. The Welsh people are
most kind & hospitable & we can get most things very
easily. A home-made CAKE would be very pleasant. I
hope this will be posted in L'pool to-morrow morning.

Yr. loving sons,
George and Trafford

Pythagoras House
Cambridge
May 21, 1909

My dear Mother,

I have excellent news of you, which delights me. You must
be very strong to have got over it so well. I suppose you
are still rather confined in your movements & employments
in bed but I hope you are beginning to feel again.

Some of the enjoyments of life – reading books! talking to
people a little anyway! Possibly you are sometimes able to
feel pleased that the sun is shining into your room and that
there hangs about your bed the scent of flowers. I am just
going to the market to see if I can get some lilies of the
valley or what shall it be! So that I may be there too.

Cambridge is flourishing and the lesson progresses slowly,
but I think not badly. I am going away for the weekend to
a Captain Farrar who lives in a pleasant place near Bidford:
he was with us in Wales at Easter for a few days. Geoffrey
Young will be there too & other Alpinists so we shall have
no doubt a good deal of talk about the mountains.

With much love & good wishes
Yr. loving son
George

The market was rather hot & unattractive & I was persuaded to buy a few roses – much against my will because the sweet peas looked so glorious.

Hôtel-Pension Bel-Alp
Tuesday, August 10, 1909

My dear Mother,

Your letter has just arrived here, I am very glad you are getting on so well. We came back from the Concordia Hut yesterday having climbed the Jungfrau in the morning. It was rather a bad day & we were snowed upon on the way up, but luckily the clouds cleared off just as we reached the summit & we had a wonderful stormy view. There has been a horrible accident to two Swiss men on the Jungfrau, a most grisly affair – no doubt you will see all about it in the English papers: there seems to be no explanation of all the facts, but the climb they were doing was well known to be a dangerous (as distinguished from difficult climb), and I expect they found the snow in bad condition & did not quite know how to deal with it. I hear also that Tatham, the Eton master, who incidentally was a great friend of Benson's has been killed climbing alone at Chamonix – it is a very curious thing if it is so, as he was not a good enough mountaineer to do that kind of thing & not a bad enough one, I understand, not to have known pretty well what he could do.

You will see on the map where we went yesterday from the Concordia, ascending the Jungfrau on the south side & back again to the Concordia Hut, a small hotel really, since one has a bed there & has food cooked for one by an attendant, down the long Ewigschneefeld, & from there to Bel Alp by the huge Aletsch glacier.

Last Saturday we traversed the Finsteraarhorn, a very noble peak and the highest in the Oberland. One goes from the Concordia over a pass called the Grünhornlücke then up to the right striking the long south arête rather high up. This was in bad condition when we were there and [it] took us a long time. We came down to the Hügisattel & then down snow slopes & up again over the Grünhornlücke & we were out altogether 17 hrs – a long day.

Our best expedition so far was a new ascent of the Nesthorn by the arête joining it to the Unterbachhorn, which we did last Wednesday. We were out 21 hrs & were altogether rather pleased with ourselves as we started in bad weather which afterwards cleared up beautifully, the sunset from the Nesthorn was the most wonderful I have ever seen, the valleys being full of grey & purple clouds & the great snow peaks standing out above them.

I wonder if you'll be able to follow all this. I hope so.

It is very sad news that Trafford should have mumps. I'm afraid he'll be rather miserable after a few days in bed.

Much love, ever yr loving son,
George

We go to Hotel Couttet, Chamonix, France to-morrow.

Pythagoras House
Cambridge
July 23, 1909

My dear Mother,

Thank you very much for the cheque which you sent
yesterday for Avie's expenses; it will be very useful just at this
moment when I have to pay vast sums to everybody it seems.

Avie I think enjoys being here, & it is very nice having her.

The rucksack came all right. Can you conjure here the
boiler in the same manner – it must be in the pantry
I think. I go to the Alps on Thursday, spending a night in
London on the way – so it ought to arrive on Tuesday if
possible as I may have to start rather early on Wednesday.

To see the Alps again! How glorious it will be – after
dreaming of them for four years.

Please give my love to Aunt Annie & my duty to Alice
whose picture I still treasure which she gave me my first
term at Cambridge – and the appropriate phrase to the
Godalming people if you see them. Much love.

Much love.
Ever your loving son,
George

2

TEACHER, DREAMER, DANDY, FATHER (1910–1915)

George decided not to follow his father into the family trade. Instead of the cloth, he settled on a career of teaching. Charterhouse, alongside Winchester another of the original seven great public schools, took him on, and he taught its boys history, maths, Latin and French.

Some aspects of the job he loved. He also expressed frustrations with it to his mother. He railed to her about 'the mechanical atmosphere of this institution', and confessed to 'moments of doubt'. Teaching wasn't George's natural calling, but he told her it stimulated him, plus it allowed him to keep up his academic pursuits, including a biography of James Boswell (which unfortunately didn't sell).

Inspirational and empathetic, George was the antithesis of the strict public-school master. His pupils liked him, none more so than the poet Robert Graves. The pair became friends, and George would be Graves's best man at his wedding. While at Charterhouse, George's dalliance with the Bloomsbury Set continued, and deepened. In one letter home, he revealed that the Post-Impressionist painter Duncan Grant had stayed with him the previous weekend, sharing only that it was 'interesting' and 'he is to paint some pictures for me'. That barely scratched the surface of it all.

George's muscular and athletic figure, his sculpted face and clear blue eyes made him the perfect artist's model. During 1911 and 1912, Duncan Grant produced a series of homoerotic paintings and photographs of George naked. Another Bloomsbury painter, Simon Bussy, also painted George, and both artists' works now hang in the National Portrait Gallery.

Avowedly rejecting the strictures of bourgeois Victorian Britain to prioritise art and beauty instead, the Bloomsbury Set were sexually bold and extremely polygamous. George too indulged. At various times, he is rumoured to have had homosexual affairs with James Strachey, the author Lytton Strachey's younger brother, and Geoffrey Keynes, as well as Duncan Grant himself, though he always fought off Lytton Strachey's own very determined lustings. 'Mon dieu! George Mallory!' Strachey wrote to Virginia Woolf. 'My hand trembles, my heart palpitates, my whole being swoons away at the words.'

Unsurprisingly, George's complicated sexuality and resulting entanglements are one side of his life he chose not to share with his mother, the country vicar's wife. Yet it was a secret the family were not unaware of.

In May 1914, George stunned his family by declaring he was to marry a woman they hadn't even met. 'What bliss! And what a revolution!' George tells his mother. '<u>Ruth Turner</u> – she lives over the river from here in a lovely house with lovely people, and she's as good as gold and brave and kind and sweet. What more can I say? I fixed it up this morning.'

George's father, Reverend Herbert, writes a lovely and revealing letter to his wife Annie the very next day: 'I am delighted about George – sly old bachelor – one always thought he was proof against feminine charms!'

Ruth and George met at a dinner party in 1913, when he was 27 and she was just 21. She was the daughter of the Arts and Crafts architect Hugh Thackeray Turner, a close friend of the movement's leader William Morris. The family lived in an elegant mansion near Godalming. Mr Turner invited George to join him and his three daughters on a family holiday in Venice, where he and Ruth fell in love. They married on July 29th, 1914, the day after the outbreak of the First World War.

At the time George wrote a letter that has recently emerged elsewhere to Lytton Strachey – by now a good friend – to qualify the developments: 'It can hardly be a shock to you that I desert the ranks of the fashionable homosexualists (and yet I am still in part of that persuasion) unless you think I have turned monogamist. But you may be assured that this last catastrophe has not happened [. . .] probably nobody is monogamous.'

A year later, in September 1915, George and Ruth's first

child was born – a daughter they named Clare. Two more children followed; a second daughter, Beridge (known to the family as Berry), in 1917 and a son, John, in 1920.

Though he can't quite bring himself to refer to Clare as more than an 'it', George's paternal pride effervesced in a charming letter to his mother about the big arrival: 'A line to tell you about the baby. It's not ugly. The colour is quite beautiful, it has a delicately formed little mouth and ears. Its forehead doesn't bulge and its cheeks aren't flabby. In fact it's quite an attractive little object.'

Domesticity, as George was learning, also had its appeals.

Neerwys
Charterhouse
September 25, 1910

My dear Mother,

Thank you for sending the parcel of washing. I am not very confident however that all my clean clothes were sent – a green shirt & some handkerchiefs are missing. I feel pretty sure that the former went to the wash at home. I have found my cheque book; it was in my writing case as I had always thought, but I had looked there twice & failed to find it because it was in an envelope of different shape to that retained in my imagination. I feel a beast for bothering you all – former losses have made me anxious.

I am enjoying life here, though there are moments of doubt. My work is a good deal with small boys who are much more difficult both to teach & to control, but it amuses me & that is the great thing – dreariness is fatal to success in teaching & if I escape that I may learn how to be of some use.

I came here on Wednesday. I have a pleasant room on the ground floor, & my bow window looks towards the South. I have bought a lot of furniture – I even had to buy a bed – I wonder if you will think I was wise; I got the cheapest bed & the most expensive mattress provided by Godalming. By the bye I think I could do with another blanket if you have one to spare – at least, I shall want one for the winter. Also, I would be very glad to have the *table linen – I always understood that it was given to me by you & partly by Gra (her own table cloths) when I went to Cambridge. I was surprised to find some plate in the box after all & very glad. Thank you. Yes – I think we shall want some more knives & I will buy those off you if they are good ones. My bookshelves I left behind till I should know if I would want them. I don't at present, as I have had some made to fit into recesses on either side of the fireplace – & they with a single long shelf which I had at Cambridge **poised** on a wall, will be sufficient. The table, truth to tell I forgot about – very humiliating under the circumstances. I am pleased with my room – white paint on the wall distempered a dead grey colour which I begin to like very well. My old furniture looks very well in it – an oak settle, a small one with square panels in the back & whose seat is the lid of a convenient receptacle; three old arm chairs – two of them have rush seats, which will give you an idea of the kind of thing, & the other which is of the same order of furniture only with a stuffed seat [&] is of a particular splendour & breadth wh. marks it for a 'drunkard's chair'_– etc – it will take you too long if I give you an inventory – I bought a chest of drawers – it is made of oak, is of a certain age, not a bad looking thing in fact 'very good value' at £2.10, but too small to

* particularly napkins.

be really convenient. I think I shall demand my sea-chest of you sometime if I am to stay on here.

Now I must end. Much love to you all & please thank Mary for her letter.

Y[our]. v. affect[ionate] son,
George

I forgot – somewhere or other these ought to be at home, a pair of blue shorts, a newish pair of a rather fine smooth serge; also white tennis shoes – unless Trafford stole them. And there is certainly a blue tie of knitted silk which is very precious to me. All these things I should be glad to receive – & the sooner the better.

Charterhouse
Godalming

My dear Mother,

Thank you for your letter, just arrived – I am unspeakably
busy this evening – so must defer my letter. Reviews have
just begun to appear. Very good in the Globe – but stupid –
he says I say exactly the opposite of what I do say about B
as a genius & also contradicts himself flatly.

Polly Jenkinson ran off with it this morning to show Aunt
B – & is sending it on. The Athenæum good too (I haven't
had a cutting yet) – very long, which is a great compliment,
disagrees a good deal but in a respectful manner – altogether
(considering what reviewers are) very pleasing.

Duncan Grant has been staying the weekend – very
interesting – & he is to paint some pictures for me. Last
weekend I stayed with Rendall at Winchester – most
agreeable – people apparently still glad to see me. Sorry for
the few words.

Love to all,
G.

Charterhouse
October 15, 1913

My dear Mother,

I have been more than lazy about writing, I fear. Thank
you for your cheerful letter. I don't like to hear that you are
imbibing at sulphur springs; but you seem to enjoy it.

I have been in an enterprising mood just lately – full of
schemes & energy. The mechanical atmosphere of this
institution has so much oppressed my spirit of late that
I have determined to take my courage in my hands &
give some lectures about pictures, for the edification
if it may be of a few well-intentioned philistines. This
preoccupation led me, for the weekend, of all glorious
places to Winton [Winchester].

I spent a night with the Headmaster, with much talk of
Italian Art, and a second very good night with Irving &
his wife. Yesterday was 'Cathedral Sunday' as we used to
say; you may remember that once a month the whole
school used to troop to Cathedral for evening service &
occupy the chancel; it was always a very splendid
monopoly – the town was never admitted on these
occasions – & I was proud to sit in a stall once again with
boys all round. It was a good visit altogether – a glorious
day yesterday, & to-day a pleasant return journey in a motor
car – curiously enough I met a friend yesterday who was

also down for the weekend tho' not an O.W.
[Old Wykehamist] & by his good nature I was saved a
most tiresome train journey.

I have loads of reading to do as usual. Four history pupils
have been thrust upon me. I have to slave for them.

Mary tells me that Harry may have to go to a far country
& will be away six months. Is this news confirmed?

Much love from
George

Charterhouse
Godalming
May 1, 1914

My dear Mother,

I am engaged to be married. What bliss! & what a
revolution! <u>Ruth Turner</u> – she lives just over the river from
here in a lovely house & with lovely people – she's as good as
gold & brave & true & sweet. What more can I say! I fixed it
up this morning. It was with Ruth & her family that I was
staying in Venice & it was there my own mind became
resolved.

When are you coming here – you have never said.

Yr. loving son,
George

George's father, Herbert Leigh-Mallory, reacts to the news of his son's engagement.

*

May 2, 1914

My dearest wife,

It was very nice & thrilling together on the telephone – I am delighted about George – sly old bachelor – one always thought he was proof against feminine charms! I send you Victoria's letter as she asks us to – I am glad she likes the velouté, she is very discriminating!

I <u>hope</u> your neuritis is slipping away through your fingertips, it is a weary malady.

I have had a long funeral & have a baptism, churching & evensong in view at 6. I have just finished the watering & must write a line to the bridegroom elect.

With much love,
always yr. very devoted
husband

Not one mother-in-law amongst our three matrimonially disposed offspring!

Charterhouse
Godalming
May 3, 1914

My dear Mother,

I've been so full of my own joy that I never said how sorry
I am that you are in this poor rheumatic state – I do hope
Buxton is doing you good. Here's Ruth – the only photo
I have, so please send it back very soon. It was taken some
years ago, 6 or so I think, but is very like her now – & even
the photo is wonderfully brave & true & sweet & good –
don't you think so?

Avie leaving this morning. It's been splendid having her
here just now, & she's made great friends with the Turners.

Yr. loving son,
George

Ruth sends her love

The Holt
Godalming
September 19, 1915

My Dear Mother,

Just a line to tell you about the baby. It's not ugly. The colour is quite beautiful. It has a delicately formed little mouth and ears. Its forehead doesn't bulge & its cheeks aren't flabby. In fact it's quite an attractive little object. It has already made some attempts to have a meal – these were very disgusting – accompanied by horrid sounds of sucking loudly & puffing & blowing greedily like a little pig with its nose in the trough.

Poor Ruth is thoroughly uncomfortable but quite happy. It was a very difficult birth. They say the infant could never have arrived by itself.

There was trouble after birth too. It was a hideous long time altogether; the actual birth took place about 9.30.

Goodbye. Much love,
Yr. loving son,
George

Will you send a pic. to Trafford & Doris – let me know their address.

3

THE WAR (1916–1918)

Britain declared war on Germany on August 4th, 1914. Yet for the first 16 months of the intense struggle, George played no part in it, to his considerable frustration.

Despite sharing many of the Bloomsbury Group's misgivings about the conflict, he still wanted to do his bit. His younger brother Trafford and many of his friends had joined up, but a government edict banned teachers from serving, and Charterhouse's headmaster Sir Frank Fletcher refused to accept George's special pleadings.

As the war went on, friends of George started to die, including Rupert Brooke in April 1915, whom he'd met at Cambridge. His former pupils were dying too, including four out of the twenty boys in his history class the previous year. Young men being killed so that George should live in peace in Surrey was too much for him. Without the school's permission, he persuaded his brother-in-law – Mary's husband Ralph Brooke – to get him a commission in his corps, the Royal Artillery, off the back of George's expertise in maths.

Sir Frank Fletcher eventually relented. George began training in January 1916, and was posted to France with 40th Siege Battery, Royal Garrison Artillery, in May, in time to fight in the Battle of the Somme. It was 'a gruesome experience', he admitted to his mother, while not burdening her with too many of the gory details. They probably wouldn't have got through anyway, with each of his envelopes marked with the stamp 'Field Censor'.

Life as a gunner was safer than an infantryman's, as George didn't have to go over the top, but he often went forward to the front trenches for observation work, and enjoyed watching German soldiers scuttle up and down their lines through his telescope.

By the autumn, life for George had become the predictable miserable morass. A letter home in November contains a careful description of his leaky dugout. George wrote that 'our chief occupation here lately has been to fight the rain and mud'. He also kindly thanked his mother for the warm waistcoat and crystallised ginger in her last package, but gently told her of his 'doubts of any opportunities' to use the bath salts she had also sent him.

In 1917, he fought at the Battle of Arras, but in May his frontline service was interrupted by an old ankle injury. The stress of soldiering on it had led the bone to disintegrate and made it very difficult to walk on, so he was sent back to London for a painful operation to rebuild it. He recuperated on morphine and slept with the help of 'aspirin and brandy'.

'Dreary' postings around southern England followed

his recovery, as George completed promotion and training courses, including one on surviving gas – punctuated only by the exciting arrival of a new commanding officer, one Major Gwilym Lloyd George, the wartime prime minister's younger son. He tried to cheer himself with thoughts of returning to the mountains, if he survived the war that is.

In September 1918, George was back at the front – now with 515 Siege Battery – and witnessed endgame for the broken German army. George celebrated the joy of Armistice Day in an officer's mess in Cambrai with his brother Trafford, who was stationed nearby. Wounded in the trenches in 1915, Trafford had transferred to the Royal Flying Corps and won a Distinguished Service Order as a pilot in command of his squadron.

As George's extraordinary letter home on November 15th testifies, the war had a very profound effect on everyone who fought in it. He describes its eventual end as 'a foretaste of heaven, mostly in realising the amount of good that must inevitably result from our victory'.

All that slaughter, all those lost friends, the pointlessness of the last four years, must all have been for something. But where was that good to be done? George, by now a passionate Fabian, waxed lyrical about 'this opportunity to control the activities of commercialism in all their sinister forms'. Or could there be another way he could leave his mark on a better world?

Willowdene
St Mary's Road
New Romney
April 7, 1916

My dear Father,

It's long since I heard from you & I hear that you've lost a
curate & are therefore at least very hard worked – I hope
not overworked? It is very bad luck to be short-handed just
at your busiest time; & Brooks was a good man wasn't he? I
take it you are probably alone again now, for mother talked
in her last of going off to Buxton very shortly. I have been
wondering how I shall manage to see you both before I get
sent off – if that happens, as it well may, when this episode
comes to an end. That date will be just before Easter; I
don't suppose I shall get off till the Saturday & I <u>must</u> go to
Godalming then & make a collection of camp kit etc – to be
ready if the call comes. Of course it is equally likely that I
shall get sent to a new battery in England & be training
with them for two or three months but it seems a not
uncommon fate of those who are 'on courses' here to be sent
out at a moment's notice & no leave given. If that fate were
mine it would probably happen immediately after Easter –
would you be able to come down to London then to spend
a few hours?

Life here is not unpleasant, but rather dull for Ruth—I go
into Lydd on a bike (4$\frac{1}{2}$ miles) at 8.30 & return about 6.30.

It's hardly worthwhile rushing back for lunch though I
have tried that plan. Still, our rooms are not
uncomfortable – a very bright little house & quite delightful
people; the good woman moreover is a real good cook.

This country is much flatter than the palm of one's hand or
any pancake – except for the network of dykes & the line of
hills is from 12 to 9 miles away. It is full of spacious &
beautiful churches. We visited yesterday afternoon the two
most attractive little towns imaginable – Winchelsea &
Rye. An expedition on bicycles; on a lovely spring day, &
with everything most convincingly all right with the
world. The church at Winchelsea must be the finest
specimen (outside cathedrals) of 14th century architecture
in England & the monuments the most beautiful I have
ever seen.

The place itself – I called it a little town, but that
description doesn't suit it all, for it has no streets & no
slums: it is more like a mediaeval gardened city & occupies
the top of a sweet little hill with views over the marshes on
one side & gentle downs on the other. It <u>would</u> be a place to
live! You ought to be rector there.

Rye is much more of a crowded town, the quaint old houses
all jostling for a place on the hill.

My work here is most interesting, because I spend most of
the time listening to the details of a man's experience at the

front – told of course from the professional point of view –
I can tell you there'll be plenty to do in a battery! Forward
observation is probably the most exciting part of the job &
the most dangerous. Ruth looks carefully at the casualty
lists daily & seldom sees names from the R.G.A. [Royal
Garrison Artillery] & so when I do go out, don't be too
anxious.

Love from us both,
Yr. loving son,
George

July 16, 1916

My dear Mother,

I am sadly in your debt I fear for I believe I have had two good letters from you & an excellent parcel since I last wrote. You will probably have heard from Ruth before this reaches you that I am in the area of the offensive – so you may imagine that I'm pretty well occupied. We have blazed away a wonderful lot of our 100 lb shell since the 'Push' started & it's surprising to see how great dumps of ammunition by the road side get used up. It isn't really very hard work, but it occupies a great deal of time; one is always 'standing by' to fire at this or that trench or strong place in the enemy's line, although very often in the end we may not fire where we expect & have a fresh target thrown at our heads, so to speak, according to what the infantry happen to need – we have prepared our angles & make ready for every contingency. Most of my work has been with the gun & I have been on duty alternate nights – which means that I occupy our office & map room with my ear more or less to the telephone & then when Headquarters sends us orders out I pop & see the business through. I have just come to the end of a night on duty – in fact I'm still on duty, only a signaller is in the office & I am in the mess-tent (6.30 a.m.). Last night we hadn't to fire at all – so much the worse for me – nothing to break the spell & make the time pass quickly. And then follows a day on duty when I take charge at the guns; but this doesn't imply that one does nothing on the alternate day; the chances are that if ever one begins to write a letter one is called off to work at figures in the Map Room.

This week the routine was varied by a spell of 3 days in the Observation Post – rather lonely work on a flat hilltop & not much sought after: but I rather enjoyed it. The quiet peace up there was very welcome after the infernal din of field guns down here. It is not a very comfortable spot. One has a bed of rail, if we're in a dank clay hole & for companions two signallers. If there is anything to be seen one has to be on the lookout constantly & there is a certain amount of night work. I spent quite a lot of time cooking. Your parcel came in splendidly up there; I particularly relished the gingerbread & meat cubes & bulls eyes also very good & the country pie too.

It has disappointed me that we haven't moved on yet, the part immediately in front of us has been very difficult to take, but it seems we have given the Fritz a bit of a whacking now, so we suppose we may be moving soon. It will be a gruesome experience I fear. Still, we shall be in such high spirits that we shall easily put up with – even rats. My little dugout here with its 'cupola' roof is perfectly comfortable & affords some protection from shell fire too, not that I've had occasion to need it yet in this place. We've been wonderful lucky in that way.

Much love to you & Father
Yr. loving son,
George

October 12, 1916

My dear Mother,

A very good letter from you arrived two or three days ago.
I am glad father has been able to resume his activity with
the Mission & glad he is playing such an active part; I'm
sure it will do him good & make him happy even if it is too
hard work; he will have to take things a bit easier when it
is over.

As to the waistcoat – it sounds most attractive & I think I
should like it very much. What about waiting till I am
home on leave – I'm hoping that will be anyway before
Xmas – & I could then see that it fits. That would be soon
enough for the real cold weather & meanwhile I hope to
keep warm in a woollen one which Ruth sent me the other
day. But if it is a case of getting it now or never it would be
wise to allow 37ins for chest measurement & something less,
I should say about 31 for the tummy.

I'm glad to hear good news of Trafford; I owe him a letter
& haven't heard for some time. I had a very good letter
from Avie which came with yours; she seems very cheerful
& gave me a most amusing account of the whimsicalities
of John.

I'm having a very slack time just now. Two days ago the
Captain took me into Amiens – quite a joy ride. The

battery is divided now into two sections & Lithgar himself
lives in the only available dugout with the 'left half' to
which I belong & does most of the work – and in the fluid
state of the battle just now it hasn't seemed worthwhile to
dig any more accommodation up there, so four of us (one
officer is always with the right half) live very comfortably
in these old quarters where we have been for the last seven
or eight weeks & go to & fro. About one day in four or five I
visit the trenches for observation work. But that is a very
soft job compared to what it was before [when] we drove
the enemy down the hill. I rather enjoy that when things go
well. One of our guns knocked quite a good lump out of the
tower of Pys Church the other day when I was observing
& also landed several rounds into the nave. One loses all
respect for churches in the enemy's country! It's interesting
too when one sees Huns through a telescope running along
a path or popping into a trench.

We have not been favoured by the weather since the end of
last month but there ought to be some fine days to come if
the weather follows its usual course out here. I feel we must
get Bapaume before real winter conditions begin & we find
ourselves more or less clogged by mud. We have had a
sufficiently good foretaste of that already; indescribably
beastly for a pedestrian! I expect we shall get it too though
Goodness knows with what sacrifices.

I suppose America must come into the war now that the
submarine campaign has started again – under such

aggravating circumstances for the Yankees. It is simply a
political move so as to have a better excuse for making peace?

Much love to you both,
Your loving
George

Please send out the stuff you mentioned for my ankle. It is
still troublesome though better. And a parcel if you feel
inclined, they never come amiss.

November 11, 1916

My dear Mother,

Your parcel arrived some days ago – & very seasonably, for
we have had it really cold & I was delighted & kept warm
by the waistcoat; you've chosen splendidly; it's a most
comforting garment & very comely too. Many thanks also
for the two medicinal items in the parcel; I have used the
furniture polish or whatever it may be & it seems very
good; but I doubt of any opportunities here to use the salts.
The crystallised ginger was excellent & the gingerbread still
continues to be so.

Our chief occupation here lately has been to fight the rain &
mud; I feel that I know already what the winter will be like
& it's not a pleasant thought. Evidently very little can be
done under these conditions & that will perhaps be the
worst of it – that we shall have too little to do. Inactivity
will matter much less to officers than to men; we're more
comfortable than they are – there's no getting away from
that – & personally I'm in no great danger of being bored
so long as I can read & write. Still it will be a somewhat
depressing experience.

My present dugout is fairly comfortable; true, in the deluge
two days ago, it sprang no less than four leaks, & the walls
& floor are still pretty damp: but some works I have carried
out since then will I hope prevent the worst of calamities.

And then I have recently acquired an oil stove & however much it may stink & begrime my pillow I know it for a cosy friend & it will learn clean habits. At this moment I am sitting at my table which is covered by a very pretty green & red tablecloth & carries a quite typical strew of books & papers – or rather it is apt to do so; at present my neat little piles are irreproachable. The bed occupies quite one third of the floor space; but I have managed to fit in my canvas armchair and a stool near my bedside takes more books, and, when I am in bed, an oil lamp. High above the head of my bed is a shelf for the hairbrush, toothbrush etc. Washing takes place outside & is apt to be a chilly occupation; the great difficulty is to keep one's feet out of the mud, & there's too much standing on one leg while one washes & dries the other.

The war seems too depressing to talk of just now; the bad weather out of season has spoilt our chances on this front; & the enemy's effort against Roumania is a surprising marvel which augurs no good for the future. No news of leave yet; I can hardly hope to get back long before Xmas – perhaps not till after that. I forget to say thank you for the slipperettes – they are very comfy with gum boots.

Much love to you both,
Yr. loving son,
George

May 20, 1917

My dear Mother,

My immediate future is settled now. I am in a hospital in
London & am to be operated on on Tuesday morning. It
sounds a queer arrangement to be occupying a bed in a
hospital so soon; but that had to be because my great man
Openshaw was so slow that my leave expired before he had
done anything & one has to be attached to a hospital in
order to stay in England.

It's a very nice place – a very fine private house in civil
life – 38 Queen Anne Street – just in the thick of the swell
doctors; the staff seem to be charming people – evidently
I shall be very comfortable.

I'm afraid it is quite useless trying to make any plans at
present – I have so little idea of what is likely to happen
to me. I expect to be here about 3 weeks but as some of the
officer patients seem already to have reached a
convalescent stage & still remain, perhaps I may be there
longer. But anyway as you see it's quite impossible to
make any plan for the future. If you could see me down
here that would be so much to the good, but there'll
surely be <u>some</u> chance afterwards. Perhaps if I get shipped
off to some convalescent home that would be the best
opportunity of all.

It has been very pleasant in the country down at
Westbrook, though the time has been rather interrupted by
visits to London & XRay photos. The ankle seems to have a
number of diseases, in fact it is described as a very
interesting right ankle. The doctor talks of synostosis of the
fibula & ankylosis between that same important bone with
the astragalus – the result being tenosynovitis in more than
one tendon. Clearly speaking two bones are stuck together &
the tendons have been doing too much work. The operation
will be on Tuesday morning.

Much love to you both,
Your loving George

May 23, 1917

My dear Mother,

I was delighted by the tulips which arrived this morning –
they <u>are</u> lovely ones – beautifully fresh.

This is evidently going to be a painful business. When a
fierce man has taken a large chisel & driven it through one's
ankle with a mallet one must expect to feel something. And
the worst of it is that he will begin moving it about in ten
days' time to prevent the bones reuniting.

Well, I suppose I shall be a strong man at the end of it; &
meanwhile the folk here as nice as can be & quite disposed
to give me morphia when I want it – which happily I have
resisted so far. I got 3 hrs sleep last night on aspirin &
brandy!

Much love,
Your loving George

Lisowen
Camberley

December 11, 1917

My dear Mother,

No doubt you have heard from Mary since writing your letter to me. Her cold was very bad & took a long time to mend, but she had already decided, when your letter came, to see her doctor, & his visit seemed to mark the turning point; she was very much better when I saw her on Saturday & Ruth says the cold didn't seem to be bothering her to-day. It has been very nice to see so much of Mary – she always seems cheerful & full of talk; but I expect she does feel a bit despondent at times when no one is with her.

I am now attending a 'Gas Course' in Aldershot – a loathsome business but very necessary in these times & there are only four days of it. I frankly dislike sticking my head into a flannel bag stiff & sticky & stinking with chemicals; the box respirator though a better device can be very disagreeable; at these places of instruction many people use these objects & the respirator I had yesterday was in a positively filthy condition so that I was nearly sick. The formation of the battery proceeds very slowly & the training has scarcely begun yet – we shan't be busy till it is in full swing. Meanwhile I have been recommended for a 'Battery Commanders' course' – quite a good thing in itself;

but what may happen after that I can't tell; I might be sent out right away or I might return here to the battery. I expect that to begin after Xmas; it will take me away from here & away from Ruth – probably to Lydd.

We shall get over to Godalming for Xmas I expect. But it's not likely to be a very bright occasion; the wonderful thing is that we are not all far more gloomy than we are.

The Russian news however seems better to-day & one thing at least is certain that the radical Bolsheviks can't possibly fix up peace with imperialist Germany & the effort to do so may both discredit the German government with their own people & convince the Russians that the Allies are right in going on.

Much love to you both,
Your George

Penclawdd
Farnborough Park
Hants

February 10, 1918

My dear Mother,

I fear it's been a long interval 'this time' – the fact is I've been so depressed that I haven't felt like writing to anyone. The wearisomeness of this stupid little job has had the best of me lately, to be condemned in these times to do about $\frac{1}{16}$ of a man's job & spend most of the day over it takes all the life out of me. However I've looked up these last days. I've now started running before breakfast & I think that's very good for me; it's heartening too to find my ankle strong enough & I think there's really a prospect of it becoming almost as strong as it ought to be one of these days for the fine feelings of athletic performance – a small matter perhaps, still I look forward to the mountains once again if I survive the war.

Ruth & I made an expedition yesterday to Bentley, it is rather more than 10 miles by road & Ruth hadn't yet attempted so long a distance on her bicycle, but she's in splendid form now & seems equal to everything. There has been a S.W. gale blowing here off & on for the last three days & after struggling to Farnham we took the train to Bentley. We found that Aunt Annie & Alice had gone to a festivity at the village school – Aunt A. apparently the most important figure, as president, though I didn't make out over what or whom she presided. I thought her looking very well & happy & she seemed to have lots of vitality – What a talker she is! Alice seemed happy too – she looks a good deal older than when I used to go there for 'leave-out' from Winton. We found their garden full of aconites & snowdrops & hellebores, very pretty, & a general air of prosperity about the place, warm & richly soiled I should think it must be.

We saw Mary on Friday – she was to go to Lydd yesterday. She has picked up splendidly just lately, looks well & very pretty & says she has no signs of indigestion. It is a great thing she has this new nurse, a mercy for which she feels very grateful to you. She's evidently a nice woman & Mary likes & trusts her – a much more capable person than Susan was.

Our two are both very well. Clare had a week at Westbrook, where everyone adores her & returned here on Friday. She's looking splendid just now & is developing beautiful eyes.

Much love from us both,
Your loving son,
George

Hant Town Mers
Lydd
June 4, 1918

My dear Mother,

You will have been wondering how the change of scene
from Aldershot to Lydd has presented itself to me during
the past fortnight. The great thing is that I am now
fervently occupied & instead of wondering how to pass
the hours of working day it is a question of how possibly
to fit the work into the hours. We were almost filled up
with recruits 10 or 12 days ago – excellent men, so that
one quite enjoys training them. That is in itself a good
sign – that we should receive drafts of men – it shows
that the authorities regard us with favour; and indeed a
good many favourable comments have been made about
us & it seems now to be decided – a consummation we
have all hoped for – that we should go out as a battery &
not be split up.

And there has been a crowning mercy – just before leaving
Aldershot we lost our major – a just & good man, a good
gunner & a gentleman, but withal too heavy a bore to be
supported even by my patience.

Not many days ago a new major appeared upon the
scene; we all like him; he gives us complete responsibility
for anything we have to do & is not in the least pompous.

But it seems that he is not yet fit for general service, & we may be ready to go out before he is so there is some chance that we shall have another change; last night it was announced as a 'fait accompli' that Major Lloyd George had been posted to us; he's very young but quite competent I believe & pleasant; if he has as many brains as his father we should at least lead an exciting life with him.

Meanwhile there is no talk of leave & one wouldn't want it. It is quite certain I believe that leave will come when our course of training ends & we mobilise, i.e. receive our guns & stores etc before embarking.

It is amusing that I should found myself here with regard to Ralph in statu pupillari. He criticised our first shoot on Saturday & gave a very good little talk about it, which quite delighted all the other officers who felt that it was friendly criticism & not the too common type of 'strafing' which prevails too often on such occasions.

I took a shoot myself this morning. R. was down to superintend it & another I.G. [Instructor Gunnery] took his place; I can't help thinking R. got out of it in case he should have the task of calling me over the coals if I did badly – as a matter of fact my part of the show went quite well. It is quite a pleasure to be firing off guns again after this long period of comparative inertia.

Ruth will have told you the other part of my life at present – I must now go on parade.

Much love to you both
Your loving son,
George

Friday, October 4, 1918

My dear Mother,

It must now be a week since Ruth left you so you can have had no news since we came up the line. This is a truly amazing life. We found ourselves suddenly at the base pitched into a number of trucks, which with our gun & ammunition wagon made up the train to take us forward, but these trucks are not merely for conveyance; they are our present & future home. We stopped that night in a railway station after a wet day's journey & there or very near there we have since remained. A noisy & too public a place for my liking. Half our life is spent on the platform, which is our cookhouse, bathroom & promenade. But the trucks are in many ways excellent accommodation. We shall have no shipping up & down the muddy steps of a dugout, no struggle to keep the water out (the roofs are sound) & no rats so long as we inhabit them. They are however exceedingly cold. The floor boards are often separated by ½ an inch or more & the sliding doors in the middle of each side seem to be designed to accommodate the most violent streams of air; and it will be difficult to arrange fires. But we're going to be wonderfully comfortable. At present the battle has left us behind; we are waiting for a line to be laid in land not long vacated by the enemy.

I suppose you have been thrilled as I have been by the wonderful news of this last week. The Hun is not broken

yet but his bones must be aching sorely. If only we could
have a month's fine weather I feel that much might still be
done this year. The great thing is that he should have the
winter to fare with the knowledge that his best defences
have collapsed & the feeling that nothing he can do can
prevent the inevitable end. I wish we could bring in
Roumania again & really get the upper hand in Russia.

I'm very glad Ruth went to you from Newcastle & I've no
doubt you were glad of an energetic pair of hands as well as
her company.

Much love to you both. Your loving son George. I'm afraid
Trafford is about 25 miles from me.

November 15, 1918

My dear Father,

I wonder how you have been feeling during these last few days? Isn't it an incredible joy! I think we can hardly have realised before how the lead was always pressing down our hearts. Now at last we seem to have received a wonderful freedom, a wonderful healing in which all harshness of overtried nerves & all unkindness of our war-weary spirits are soothed into gentleness & love. We can never thank God enough; & can we ever live nobly enough to be worthy of such a gift? Life presents itself very much to me as a gift; if I haven't escaped so many chances of death as plenty of others, still it is surprising to find myself a survivor – and it's not a lot I have always wanted; there has been so much to be said for being in the good company of the dead. Anyway it's good to be alive now, partly because this gigantic struggle has been worthwhile; we haven't fought for any flag-wagging jingoism, nor for any remote & material political aim but simply to have a better world to live in; as one who had an almost embittered sense of the violence done continually on every hand to all that we know to be best, to the elements of Christianity, by what used to be called 'the forward march of civilisation' – feeling at times positively a stranger in the world that was so detestable. It seems to have a foretaste of Heaven mostly in realising the amount of good that must inevitably result from our victory; and when I think of this opportunity I seem almost to be drinking again as I used to of an evening in Rome that amber-red Frascati wine which is the loveliest wine in the world – this opportunity to control the activities of commercialism in all their sinister ramifications – to find antidotes here & now for half the poisons in the world.

You see my generation really grew up with a disgust for the appearances of civilisation so intense that it was an ever present spiritual discomfort, a sort of malaise that made us positively unhappy. Though I don't know that I have ever put it to myself so definitely before[,] I see now that this discomfort was the essence of what may be called 'young twentieth century thought'. It wasn't that we simply criticised evils as we saw them & supported movements of reform; we felt such an overwhelming sense of incalculable evil that we were helplessly unhappy. Civilisation will leave us plenty of evil appearances & realities henceforward but the world will seem to have a chance & western civilisation may be brought into line with Christianity.

I'm afraid you will be tiring of this talk when so many beautiful human realities are at hand for our appreciation. How delighted you must be as I am that Trafford has come through the war so splendidly. I spent a night with him early this week & we celebrated peace together at Cambrai; he was bubbling over with joy & activity. He has evidently done extremely good work lately & has shown himself a person of enterprise & resource. I very much hope he may be decorated as he well deserves; but such distinctions are partly a matter of chance – the chance of being attached to an ordinary channel of recommendation & Trafford in having worked very much apart from his immediate superior officer the Wing Commander misses the best natural chance of recommendation.

I dare say you have heard that I have a good chance of returning home before so very long. I had a letter from Fletcher about a month ago asking whether he should apply for my release under an Army Council Order to the effect that schoolmasters who have been out here more than 6 months should return to their jobs if so desired & were wanted – & replied that I should like him to apply as soon as an armistice was signed. Of course I don't know what may happen but I'm inclined to think the A.C.O. will hold good, though the purpose was expressed as 'the training & education of future officers', and in that case I shall be back at C'house [Charterhouse] next term.

Much love to you both,
Your loving son
George

4

DISILLUSIONMENT AND DREAMS (1918–1921)

Demobilising six million men and getting them all back home took time. For George that meant some leave in Paris, Christmas with his soldiers in France and a white-knuckle biplane flight with one of his brother Trafford's daredevil pilots. He was put on a boat back to England in January 1919, and returned to his old teaching job at Charterhouse to try to pick up where he'd left off more than two years before.

The school, like so many others, had been decimated by the war. It lost 670 former pupils, the vast majority of them in their teens and 20s, and many as young lieutenants leading their men over the top. Of the original 60 members of the mountaineering society that George ran, 23 had been killed and a further 11 wounded.

Teaching had never been the easiest fit for George, and his post-war disillusionment didn't make it any easier. He regularly shared his continued frustrations with the strictures of public school life with his mother. As a master who liked his pupils, George confessed that he always hated losing the oldest for good at the end of the academic year. 'It is all rather depressing – the one serious drawback to this life.'

On the positive side, George delighted in being with Ruth and their children again, and back in domesticity in Godalming. He regaled with pride to his mother the improvements they were making to their house and garden. The couple's third child – the son they had long hoped for, John – arrived early in August 1920 while George was still on a much-looked-forward-to climbing trip (and after a dramatic dash home in a borrowed motor car by Ruth).

The end of war also meant that he could get back to the mountains. The riotous annual Easter trips to Pen-y-Pass in Snowdonia with bohemian friends were reinvigorated, and his beloved Alps re-opened to visitors again. George headed for Courmayeur and the south side of Mont Blanc, 'to me the most wonderful and beautiful part of the Alps'.

George also renewed his quest to make a better world. He stepped up his involvement in politics, with he and Ruth both joining the Labour Party. George also gave a lecture series to the Workers' Educational Association and made plans with friends to establish their own progressive school that would breach the still strict social divides. In addition, he joined the newly created League of Nations Union, which believed in a world government that would end all wars and became the leading light in the British peace movement.

With his eyes now scanning some farther horizon, by the end of 1920 George resolved to leave Charterhouse and search for a career in which his beliefs would be better expressed. He offered his services to the Union. They asked him to go to Ireland to file a report on the troubles there, which he did during the Christmas holidays in January 1921.

Ireland was in the grip of an ever more bloody fight for independence, thanks to the Westminster government's violent repression. A long and captivating letter portrays George's disgust with the brutality deployed by Britain's thuggish paramilitary forces, the Auxiliaries and the Black and Tans, and the daily terror that they inflicted. He reveals his sympathies were firmly with the 'Sinn Féiners', who gave him lodging, and the romance of their struggle clearly excited him. George also told his mother of a close shave of his own when the Dublin house he was staying in was raided. An Auxiliary pushed a pistol in George's face, but was talked out of searching his room and finding his seditious literature by, as George put it, 'my confident English accent'. 'The spirit of Ireland is amazing,' he concluded.

Excitement, fear, romance and challenge. Everything that appealed to George. He didn't know it then, but the farther horizon that would define his own life was just about to emerge, and it contained all four in abundance.

December 10, 1918

My dear Mother,

I had your letter in Paris where I have been spending 8 days' leave – I only returned two days ago. It has been a very interesting time there; I did a great deal of talking with French folk of all sorts whom I drew out in cafés & restaurants & found them for the most part very pleasant & friendly; it was very agreeable to hear their unsolicited testimonials to Great Britain's part in the War.

I spent a good deal of time in the Bibliothèque Nationale reading & rummaging in books which aren't easily found elsewhere, & not a little in bookshops (the ideal way of educating oneself) & some good evenings in the theatres. I love Paris & can enjoy it in the simplest fashion – merely walking along the boulevards or sitting outside the cafés at night watching the stream of people in the brilliantly lit streets.

We had very sudden orders to move yesterday & have now come down to join the left section about 10 miles from Calais – it seems like a step towards home; but I'm not feeling very optimistic about my home-coming; it is now 4 weeks since application was made for my release & I have heard nothing. I don't expect to be back for Xmas, though I still hope for that. The real tragedy will be not to get back for the beginning of next term on Jan. 17 – if that should be.

I wonder how long Mary & Ralph are to be with you? It <u>would</u> be nice all to join up.

Ruth as you have no doubt heard has got over her attempt at pneumonia in brilliant fashion – still it is a nasty dangerous sort of thing – one has heard of so many who have succumbed to it & it is hateful to be out here under these circumstances. It is splendid that both Doris & Avie should have done so well after their previous troubles.

I spent a night with Trafford on my way back from Paris; he was as bright & cheerful as ever, full of his command & his prospects; he has certainly done & is doing very well. One of his pilots took me for a fly to leave a message at the battery & stunted in the most wonderful way. I experienced the most incredible sensations & held on as I have never held on to anything in my life.

Please thank Father for his letter which I also received in Paris.

Much love to you both,
Your loving son,
George

Charterhouse
Godalming

March 16, 1919

My dear Mother,

Our ideas for Easter don't seem to fit at all. We were proposing to bring the children to see you. My holidays begin on the 11th & we thought of coming up about then & staying till 15th & 16th when we are fixed to go to Pen y Pass for a week – there is to be a large reunion of climbers after which we should come back to you for a little & go south again. After all, so far as dates go it wouldn't fit so badly, because if we carried out that scheme you could still get away a week or ten days after Easter. I wish we could join you after that, but I'm afraid I <u>must</u> get back here. Term begins about May 1 & if I don't go on teaching during the summer I shall want to get to my writing at once. Please let us know if you can have us anyway – though I fear from what you say of domestic difficulties you will hardly want us then.

Our household is getting on very nicely – our maid has turned over a new leaf & is doing well, and the children are full of life & spirits. Please thank Father for his letter which I will answer shortly. He'll be interested to hear that we've been very active in the garden. The top beds all tidied up ready for sowing, the paths weeded & the ponds cleaned out. And we have made a good start with a pergola below the loggia, which has been rather amusing work as we have had to level a bed & build a dry wall.

I had a very pleasant little visit to Trafford & Doris the other day & was much taken with Tom. I wish I had a boy!

Ruth sends very much love with mine to you both.

Your loving son,
George

July 18, 1920
The Holt
Godalming

My dear Mother,

This has been a particularly long gap; one way and another I seem to have had my hands overwhelmingly full. The time when boys begin to revise for examinations is usually a comparatively empty one; but this term it has involved a lot of special work, often in the evenings with boys who have been promoted during the year into my forms & haven't covered the ground. And then I've had two large extra irons in the fire – a series of 12 lectures which I am to give to the Workers Educational Association at Farnham in the autumn & of which they require a syllabus beforehand; and an attempt I've been making to get the Union of the League of Nations to move in the matter of getting in touch with teachers in a thoroughgoing manner – this however has led to nothing at present as the Union is sadly short of funds.

I was very glad to get your letter & to hear of your holiday life. I'm afraid father made a bad start having to go up for Tom Greig's funeral, and I suppose the Greigs will be upset by his death – had he been ill long?

I've seen nothing of Trafford all this summer alas! I'm sure it's very good for him to have a quiet time in the country sometimes, & above all fishing – he lives rather a restless life I should think; but I gather he likes it well enough.

We've had a very bad patch of weather down here though this last week has been better. I hope you have had better luck. I was hoping to have seen Mary & Ralph the other day at the Varsity match, but the rain prevented play and they didn't even turn up at the rendez-vous.

Ruth is bearing her formidable burden nobly & keeps well & cheerful – wonderfully so on the whole; during the last few days however she has been much troubled by a very nasty sty in her eye.

The children have been beautifully fit & jolly since they came back from Trearddur. A friend of ours, Kennington, has been trying to make a picture of them. He stayed a week with us a made a great number of drawings & after working at his picture in London came down to have another look at them. He seemed doubtful if he would really make good likenesses & when I saw the picture I felt very doubtful too – but it is not fair to judge a half-finished picture & he is so clever that I have great hopes he will make a success of it in the end.

I am starting for the Alps at the end of this week – the earliest possible moment so as to be able to get back with a comfortable margin of time before Ruth's event. I hardly thought if would be possible to go out this year, but she so insisted that she would not be anxious & that she would be miserable if I didn't go that it has been arranged. Reade, a middle-aged member of the A. C. [Alpine Club] who is both very skillful & very careful, Elliott who came out with me last year & had to go back with water on the knee, & David Pye are coming with me & we ought to be a very strong party. We shall make Courmayeur (Hôtel Savoie, Courmayeur, Val d'Aosta, Italy) our base. That south side of Mont Blanc & the great peaks near it is to me the most wonderful & beautiful part of the Alps, & if we have fine weather we ought to have a splendid time.

The Westbrook household is away just now. Mildred is settled into her temporary home in Farnham & the others have gone away so as to give the servants a holiday. It seems rather a pity that no one should be living there even for so short time during the summer – I went up there this afternoon & found the garden looking simply lovely.

I always hate the end of this term – so many boys leave whom I have got to know and like & it is all rather depressing – it's the one serious drawback to this life.

Please give my love to Father. I hope you'll both be much better for your holiday.

Your loving son,
George

The Holt
Godalming
August 22, 1920

My dear Mother,

Thank you for your wire.

I arrived back yesterday to be met with the news that the
baby had been born only an hour before – 10 days early &
quite unexpected. R. felt the first pain about 7 a.m. &
Marjorie woke up a neighbouring household, the Williams,
by climbing in at their bathroom window with the aid of a
ladder she secured & got them to motor R. up here. She
arrived here about 9 – the maids were still in bed, & the
baby was born about 1. A local nurse was obtained until the
engaged woman should arrive, which she managed to do
about an hour before the birth. Considering the
circumstances this was less of a muddle than might have
been expected & the house seemed to be more or less in order
for the event when I arrived. But it was a difficult birth and
R. would have been saved some trouble if the proper nurse
had been here from the start. She was tired & overexcited
yesterday but has had a good night & seems very bright &
well this morning.

We're both delighted to have a son. As we've arranged no
name for him, he is to he called Hugh pro tem & perhaps
that name will stick to him.

<u>Later</u>. After a talk with R. we incline towards John or perhaps John Oliver, which sounds very fine; or perhaps to keep the family name he might be John Leigh or John Trafford. I rather like the repeated Leigh & a boy ought to be named after his grandfather ceteris paribus & neither of us like Herbert.

I had such a good sleep last night after rather a strenuous time – I had only slept once in a bed during the past week & then only for 5 hours. It was not a good season in the Alps – storms & snow every 4 days or so, just enough to spoil things, & when we first got out there it was worse than that. Still it was a very good time in all. I had five first rate expeditions including a traverse of the Matterhorn from the Italian side. And I'm wonderfully fit now.

I have a lot of letters to write & communications to make à propos of the infant so I'll write no more at present.

Much love to you both,
Your loving son,
George

The Holt
Godalming
January 26, 1921

My dear Mother,

Here I am back again in full swing much ashamed that
I haven't let you know my movements before this. I was
heartily glad to get back from Ireland – interesting as it
was. I saw a good deal altogether, though more of Sinn
Féiners than others – perhaps that was inevitable as there
are so many of them. In Cork particularly all seemed to be
of that way of thinking, the big business people who used
to be Unionists included. In Dublin half the people I knew
were more or less 'on the run' & lived the most hazardous &
exciting lives; at any time they may be stopped in the
streets & searched by Black & Tans & any night their
domiciles may be raided.

The house where I was staying was raided the last night I
was in Dublin – very wildly by 'Auxiliaries' (i.e. ex-officers
whose corps contains both the worst & the best), one of
whom came into my bedroom about 1 a.m., flashed a
torchlight in my eyes & covered me with a revolver while he
asked a number of questions; I had plenty of seditious
literature in the room, but my confident 'English accent'
put him off & he made no search. I was very glad of the
experience as it showed me what it must be like for nervy

people to hear the tramping of feet on the stairs & the rough bullying voices in the dead of night.

It is wonderful how steady & cheerful people are under this terror – the motor lorries full of behelmeted soldiers looking out over their loaded rifles which seem to threaten the passers by at every moment & dash recklessly about the streets day and night & make a terrifying noise. In Cork people had constantly been held up in the streets often robbed by the Black & Tans & sometimes maltreated – the worst of this was before the fires but it went on afterward & yet they walked about thronging the streets with the utmost cheerfulness up to the hour of Curfew.

My whole impression both from hearing stories, verifying some of the worst by talking to those who had suffered, & discussing the whole situation with men of reasoned judgement is that the excesses of our coercive policy are infinitely worse than anyone could imagine from the English or even from the Irish press. But Martial Law has tended to prevent the worst crimes & does tend to make people responsible for what they do – the trouble is that the govt is bound to continue using agents who have become, or who have been deliberately brutalised & short of murder & arson there can be no effective control over them. The greater part of the soldiers behave well, but the R.I.C. (both Black & Tans & Auxiliaries) are capable of any devilry & willing enough in any dirty work. The most shocking business is brutal treatment, even torture of men arrested;

this takes place as a rule in guard rooms & prison before
trial & is carried out I believe by men of low character
especially selected for the purpose.

The 'Murder Gang' is an invention – at least, it is a gang of
100,000 or more & I heard on all sides that these are the
finest young men in the country. I know this sounds
paradoxical & it is rather difficult to explain without going
into historical details, but the plain fact is that the killing of
policemen who are armed political agents acting as
informers was considered as a defensive measure necessary
after 4 years of govt aggression – arrests & deportations
without trial of the most provocative kind. The justice of
this plea depends upon historical facts. But in many case it
puts a different complexion upon the whole matter & many
who have been against physical force will not condemn its
use because they feel that the plea is just, at bottom, that
rebellion in fact was justified. In any case I feel convinced
that the Volunteers are acting from patriotic motives &
whatever wrong they may have done is more than balanced
by what has been done in our name. And I'm certain the
coercive policy is as futile as it is wicked. The spirit of
Ireland is amazing & no possible way can succeed in
coercing it short of confining the majority of the population
in concentration camps.

I must write no more now. Please show this to anyone
whom it may interest. Literature may be obtained from the
Peace with Ireland Council. So Queen Anne's Chambers,

SW1 – I particularly recommend 'Who burnt Cork City', of which I have satisfied myself on the spot that its contents are substantially true.

All here very well & happy.

Much love to you both,
Your loving son,
George

5

THE FIRST
EXPEDITION (1921)

The first concerted British exploration of Mount Everest came in the summer of 1921. It was a thoroughly colonial affair, and the driving force behind it – Sir Francis Younghusband – was a thoroughly colonial figure. He led the British expedition to Tibet (a de facto invasion) in 1904, and coveted the mountain's summit ever since.

Everest remained the last great adventure on the planet once the North and South Poles had been reached in 1909 and 1911 respectively. Younghusband was determined that triumph would be British.

Standing at 29,035 feet, Everest was designated the world's highest mountain in 1852 by the Great Trigonometrical Survey of India. The vast mapping project was led by the Surveyor-General, Sir George Everest, and the mountain was named after him – though Tibetans had long called it Chomolungma, 'Goddess Mother of the World'.

Planning for the first expedition began before the First

World War, but was suspended with the outbreak of hostilities. Sir Francis Younghusband was appointed chairman of the Royal Geographical Society in 1919, and planning resumed with the formation of the Mount Everest Committee in early 1921, which he also chaired. A budget was set for it at £6,000.

George, who was considered to be the best mountaineer in the country at the time, was a natural inclusion on the expedition. Over lunch in his club, Sir Francis pressed him to join it as one of its four expert climbers. George initially hesitated, as he didn't share Sir Francis's jingoism and also feared another long separation from Ruth and the children. The extraordinary challenge that Everest presented, plus the temptation of glory, allowed friends to persuade him. Ruth was among them, and she also argued that the likely resulting fame would help George in his search for a new career. Who knows, if he did get to the top, talking and writing about the heroic feat could be a new career in itself. In February 1921, George gave Charterhouse his notice, and began to prepare.

The expedition, ill-advisedly as it turned out, favoured experience over youth. Half of its nine members were in their 50s, making 34-year-old George its second-youngest member. He was also new to the Everest cause and had never been to the Himalayas before, unlike the party's most experienced climber, the 52-year-old Dr Alexander Kellas, who as a chemist had carried out physiological studies in the region on climbing with oxygen at very high altitudes.

What George did have in common with the others was he was a war veteran seeking purpose. Of the 26 total members of the three different Everest expeditions of the early 1920s, 20 had fought in the war. Six had been severely wounded, two had almost been killed by disease and two had lost brothers in the trenches. Wade Davis, author of the masterful book about the 1920s expeditions *Into the Silence*, describes Everest's meaning to them as 'a sentinel in the sky, a destination of hope and redemption, a symbol of continuity in a world gone mad'. Death also mattered less to the war veterans as they feared it less, having already seen so much of it. What was important now was how they lived.

The committee had intended for the expedition to be in two parts: the 1921 trip would hope to discover a route to the top, and a subsequent one would attempt an assault on the summit. But opinions in the group were split, and that created 'a certain amount of friction', as George put it. Some of them – George included – wanted to make a summit attempt there and then. It was eventually agreed that one would be attempted but only if a safe opportunity emerged.

George left for India from the port of Tilbury, Essex, on April 8th, 1921, onboard the steamer SS *Sardinia*. The other expedition members had gone out ahead of him as George had to wait until the end of his final Charterhouse term – much to his regret during the four-week passage. As the ship neared Malta, George told his mother about his nightly dining companions: 'I sit between an elderly colonel whose prevailing method of conversation is to apply a sledgehammer to every idea thrown out for talk [. . .] and on the other side a fellow creature indeed but one hard to be recognised as such because he doesn't utter a single word.'

The long 362-mile trek to Everest's foothills began from Darjeeling in May. The expedition had to approach the mountain that bordered two countries from its northern side in Tibet, as the fiercely independent kingdom of Nepal was closed to foreigners. It was an enormous logistical challenge. Everything – food, water, equipment, tents – had to be hauled with them, with the help of 40 porters and 100 mules. In all, this amounted to 20 tonnes of equipment, including several crates of champagne and the party's hunting guns. The porters were hired from among the local population living on the Tibetan plateau. On occasion, George also refers to the porters as 'coolies', in the dismissive and outdated colonial language of the time that does crop up in his letters. But he also exalts their courage and stamina, calling them 'a fine lot of men'. It's not the only outdated language that George uses to describe some of the people he encountered on his journeys through India and Tibet; as much as he was a social revolutionary and reformer, George was also a product of his age. That's why we decided to leave his at times uncomfortable language in place, as it's a historical document of those times.

As the members trekked through the dusty and rocky plains in knickerbockers, puttees and tweeds, they painted watercolours and collected butterflies. They cut a staggeringly eccentric picture even for observers at the time. On seeing a photograph of them, the playwright George Bernard Shaw quipped that they 'looked like a Connemara picnic trapped in a snowstorm'.

George caught his first sight of Everest from 90 miles out, through binoculars and after scrambling up a 1,500-foot hill with another of the climbers, his old friend from Winchester College, Guy Bullock. A week later, the expedition walked 'off the map', as George puts it. The closest a Westerner had come to Everest previously was 40 miles away.

Tragedy struck on June 5th with the first death of the 1920s expeditions. Dr Kellas collapsed with heart failure near the village of Kampa Dzong, weak and exhausted. The diarrhoea and dysentery that had plagued all of them had hit Kellas the hardest, not least because he had been on repeated expeditions across India throughout the previous year and had not given himself any time to recover. George told his mother and father that while he didn't know Kellas well, he was 'a man I was certain to like'. In a bid to reassure them that he was not under the same mortal threat, George also said it had become obvious that Kellas had been 'utterly unfit to come'.

Soon after, the expedition's lead climber Harold Raeburn – aged 55 – was also forced to withdraw, terribly weakened by the ardour of the journey. That left George and Bullock as the sole two remaining climbers and the job of finding a route to the summit was theirs alone.

The expedition reached Everest's foothills in mid-June. Weeks of painstaking reconnaissance followed as their quest took George and Bullock up a seemingly endless series of steep valleys and glaciers which led to insurmountable dead ends. 'Mother, this is going to be a long job. I am a little homesick,' a downhearted George confessed on July 7th. 'Perhaps the sound of the rain outside has depressed me a little tonight.'

Finally, on August 18th, they achieved breakthrough. After a gruelling nine-hour slog in heat that was 'literally like that of a furnace, burning one through the thin haze and eating one's vitality', they reached the 22,200-foot pass called Lhakpa La and at long last found a clear view of how to get to Everest's North Col, the key to climbing Everest from the north. And from the North Col, they had already observed a clear path up Everest's Northeast Ridge to the summit.

It was a colossal achievement, and George and the others in the party were elated. After 10 days of rest at base camp, they resolved to set off for the summit – but by then the monsoon had arrived and the weather turned ever worse. George and Bullock reached the North Col, but fierce gales made camping there impossible, and they were forced to turn back. The highest altitude they had reached was 23,000 feet, but a proper attempt on the summit would have to wait for next year. On September 25th, the expedition left Everest for home.

George, the eternal optimist who believed reaching the summit might have been possible before they left, was left disappointed. The sheer physical demand of the challenge had exhausted them. 'The party lost heart in the end,' he told his mother during the long passage back to England. 'There was no appetite left for the adventure, the spirit was dead.'

Without his teaching job now, or any other new career in place, George contemplated what he would do when he got home. 'The future is indeed very vague. Much seems to depend on climbing this mountain. I wonder, I wonder, shall we get up? I think of it, and can't see it's impossible – or not for me at all events.'

In George's mind now, the two were now immovably interlinked. The future was Everest.

S.S. *Sardinia*
nearing Malta
April 16, 1921

My dear Mother,

The next best thing I can do to writing to you for your
birthday is to write to you on it. The best of good wishes to
you now.

We shall reach our first port of call to-day, about noon I
hope & it will be a delightful change to get ashore for a
few hours at Malta. I can't say that I find the delights of a
voyage anything better than making the best of a bad job;
but then I'm not lucky either in the ship or in my fellow
passengers. It's a very small liner & very old (1902) & I
imagine the newest & larger ships have a good many
comforts which are lacking here. We have only one deck
for promenade & that is completely covered in so that it is
almost impossible to sit in the sun; and it is inconveniently
narrow so that there seems little enough room both for
walking & sitting & sundry feeble games even for this
small number of 1st class passengers – 43. And
unfortunately the small minority of passengers who seem
even what one would call nice people are extremely dull. I
feel very much alone & actually seek to be alone a great
deal. Fortunately, I have discovered a retreat, where so far
I have been tolerated on the one hand & unpursued on the
other – at the very point of the bows. There is a canvas

screen which keeps off the wind so that instead of sitting in a sunless funnel I bask peacefully with one silent companion, a darkie kind – Portuguese or other who stands in the bows on the lookout.

Meals are apt to be very tiresome as I sit between an elderly colonel who finds communication extremely difficult & whose prevailing method of conversation is to apply a sledgehammer to every idea thrown out for talk – him on the one side & on the other side a fellow creature indeed but one hard to be recognised as such because he doesn't utter a single word – literally he has not originated a single remark at meals since the voyage began. There is a certain naval officer's wife at our table, a light-headed young lady who at least is gay & often enlivens us & the captain at the other end makes apparently amusing talk, but he is too far away for me to hear. Two ladies including the gay one disembark at Malta, so we shall reshuffle I suppose.

I get some exercise, generally in the morning before breakfast by running furiously around the deck or skipping & by sundry exercises, & am keeping very fit. And what with reading & writing I find myself sufficiently employed.

I like myself extremely in my silk dressing gown which I use often. It was a really kind thought on your part. Thank you again.

The Mediterranean has been sparkly & lovely & the African coast good to look at. Gibraltar was very impressive at dawn & we've seen two ranges of snow-covered mountains – the Sierra Nevada & Mount Atlas. To-day the sky is overcast but I have hopes it won't rain.

I mean to see what the Knights of Malta have left there to be remembered.

Much love you both,
Your loving son,
George

Government House
Darjeeling

May 18, 1921

My dear Mother,

I had a letter from you yesterday, thank you, just in time to catch me before we start. I have just seen off the 50 mules of the first party & in 2 hrs we shall be on our way. Wollaston, Howard Bury & Wheeler will be my companions until we all join up at a place called Phari 8 days from here. Morshead has gone ahead with some Survey mules & coolies; we shall meet him at Kampa Dzong. One other man has been added to the party, Heron, a geologist, so we shall be nine in all.

I have asked Ruth to supply you with a copy of what I write in my journal or in longer letters to her, so you will hear plenty about the personnel sooner or later. It has been another trying time in some ways packing & organising here – not for me particularly, but I have observed a certain amount of friction; I expect we shall rub along well enough later.

I found myself somewhat faint-hearted on arriving here – it was not so much the heat which I stand fairly well but the constant difficulty in keeping one's tummy in order & not always succeeding in that matter. The voyage was hateful though of course it was relieved by some wonderful moments. I was most unlucky in my fellow passengers – with the exception of one kind lady who took me to stay very comfortably with her & her husband for the two days we were in Madras. Colombo was the best of what I saw on the way out – a forest-garden with highly coloured & highly scented shrubs & trees in gorgeous bloom & peopled more thickly than seems possible with dark-skinned natives most half-naked.

In Madras I become further acquainted with the East after this first glimpse and taking a long lonely walk through the native quarters which are indescribably full of teeming life – simply thick with people; I saw whole families living in tiny spaces about 6ft × 3ft, & children about Bridget's size carrying babies on their hips; and every other creature is a beggar!

In Calcutta the best sight was a large tree covered with red blossom (*Delonix regia*) about the colour of a scarlet azalea, which grows there better than almost anywhere I'm told & is the most surprising, magnificent tree imaginable, making a great solid mass of flame against the sky.

And the journey up here in the mountain railway was fascinating. They are very complicated foothills with many deep valleys & sharp edges. The hillsides are everywhere very steep & mostly wooded. One pierces the forest & gets a good idea of what it is like to be in one besides constantly seeing it from clear places outside.

Darjeeling itself is a lovely situation but spoilt by much cheap building in the suburban taste. I have seen Kanchenjunga, but it was not looking its best & I was not greatly impressed – there'll be plenty of time however for seeing mountains.

I am staying here in a Guest House attached to the main building with Wollaston & Howard Bury as co-guests. Meals are apt to be rather formal, but the cooking makes up for everything! & [illegible] I share a sitting room very comfortably.

His Excellency the Governor of Bengal seems quite a pleasant & cheery individual and an able man too I should judge. We've come in for two festivities; – a grand dinner party in honour of the expedition which happened on the night of my arrival & yesterday a garden party. I was a good deal tickled by some of the formalities.

I'm very glad to have had some days here – it has been a restful time in spite of organisation & packing our stores & I shall go on my way very fit.

It is horrible to think of what you must be going through in England with all these troubles – about which one gleans all too little out here. I hope they may be soon at an end. I wonder how you have been for coal? And what about unemployment in Birkenhead? It must be a time of great hardship to many.

In this moist climate mist is continually blowing up & we have often heavy showers of rain; so you must think of me very damp especially when we go into these deep stuffy valleys on our way through Sikhim – but that will only be for a week or so; then we shall reach & keep a higher level in Tibet.

You'll see fairly frequent news I expect in the papers & will have read of our setting forth before you get this letter.

Farewell & much love to you both.
Your loving son,
George

I shall have the little anti-insect bottle you gave me in my sack to-day.

Mount Everest Expedition
Tinkye Dzong
June 9, 1921

My dear Father,

I don't know how well you are supplied with news of me.
The weekly articles by Howard Bury in the Times is
telegraphed from Bombay & must precede my letters by
about three weeks if not more. I find it difficult to get more
than one long letter written under these conditions of life.
We usually start early for our day's march – breakfast at
6 – and the best part of the day is used up before we arrive
in camp; the transport straggles in comfortably before dusk
even on the longest days, but much time is occupied in
pitching tents in the wind and arranging things generally.
I usually occupy 2 hrs or so before dinner walking about &
seeing the place; and then dinner is a cold function & after
dinner one goes to bed.

We have not suffered greatly from cold since we got to
Kampa Dzong; but in the six days from Phari there we had
some frightfully cold winds. The keen Tibetan blast gets up
anytime between 10 & 12 & generally begins to die down
about 7. It is quite warm in the calm early morning as soon
almost as the sun strikes us, & I am quite warm enough in a
flannel shirt & coat for the upper parts to start with, but
add a Shetland sleeved waistcoat & a silk shirt against the
wind later on – a reversal of what one would expect on a

summer's day in Europe. Since we got up into the high table land at Phari we have never thought of rain & have bright sunshine continuously. We have been camping on the average at about 1500 ft & have crossed some passes of about 1700 ft or more, but on the whole it has been a flat journey from Phari crossing great gravel plains where hardly anything grows until rain comes but yellow tufts of grass & curiously enough several flowers (notably a beautiful iris & some small rock plants) which often push their way up leaving their leaves underground.

It seems that the climate in milder as we approach the Arun valley. At Kampa Dzong (Dzong mean fort) situated charmingly at the entrance of a steep valley on the edge of a great plain there was a considerable amount of cultivation & as we have come westward from there we have found a coarse grass growing in the plain quite fresh & green. The plains are everywhere backed on the south-west by low hills & beyond them surprising snow mountains. From Kampa Dzong we saw Makalu & Everest & by going up 1500 ft Bullock & I obtained a good view through glasses of the ridge joining them. Everest is only 70 miles away now, & after the next two stages we should get a very interesting view.

Transport of course is a continual problem. The 100 government mules were not a success & after a week's travelling in Sikhim were abandoned in favour of Tibetan mules – these took us very well to Phari. Since then we have had a miscellaneous assortment of animals & owing to complicated local rules they have generally to be changed at each stage. Small donkeys are generally the most numerous & yaks & bullocks make up the rest. It is a sort of living from hand to mouth & we never know whether we shall be able to get on the next day, as there may not be enough animals available in spite of the help of local authorities with whom we exchange presents (we commonly receive sheep & eggs & give electric torches). To-day for instance we are brought to a standstill only two marches from Kampa Dzong; but we shall be going on again to-morrow.

We are just entering now the really interesting part of our travels. The inhabitants of this village & the last had never before seen a European & their curiosity & excitement are immense & amusing but I'm not very fond of a crowd round the tent door; and after another march or two we shall be 'off the map' – our present map is one made at the time of the Lhasa expedition & that survey extends only a few miles further west.

Bullock & I have just been selecting coolies for the snows. They are a fine lot of men who are mostly from a region S.E. of Everest, so they belong to the mountains. They had boots fitted onto their short broad feet at Darjeeling & the business in hand now is nailing them for the mountains – a long & difficult job. In a few days' time we may have to take a party onto snow for a day in order to see Everest from the N.E. side. When we get to Tingri Dzong in about

ten days' time we shall probably form a camp up towards
Everest & make a series of exploring expeditions from there,
taking with us a dozen selected coolies & training them in
the course of these minor operations.

I haven't said a word yet of what is most on my mind to
say. You will have read of Dr Kellas's death 3 weeks or
more before you get this & I much fear that it must make
you anxious about me. The plain fact about that sad event is
that he was utterly unfit to come on this expedition. In
March & April this year he was climbing under very severe
conditions & living on insufficient food; he was a very spare
little man at any time & actually lost a stone in weight.
He had only a week for recuperation at Darjeeling before
we started & had diarrhoea there but made light of it. When
he reached Phari (he was travelling with the 2nd party; the
1st party included Howard Bury, Wollaston, Wheeler &
self) he had enteritis, due no doubt to bad food & cooking
through Sikhim before we opened our stores (everyone
except myself suffered more or less from diarrhoea & the
healthy ones have thrown it off in a normal fashion). It is
easy to see now that he should never have left Phari; but
Wollaston had no idea then of his weak state of health & it
was very difficult to make any suitable arrangement – the
calculation was that if he hadn't recovered by Kampa
Dzong he could then more easily be sent down into Sikhim
& put in the charge of a doctor; and so he was carried on &
grew daily weaker, weaker than anyone knew until as you
know he died of heart failure on the march.

It has been a very distressing event altogether. But it is not one which need cause any anxiety at home for a fit man like myself. As a matter of fact I am as fit as can be imagined – I feel as I feel in the Alps; living at this elevation makes no difference to my digestion (the all-important matter), I always have a hearty appetite & feel full of vigour. And as all depends in the end on being fit I take every possible care to keep fit & shall continue to do so.

I hardly knew Kellas. He never had a meal with us; at Darjeeling I only saw him once & in camp my connection with him went no further than occasional petits soins such as one may have for sick man. He was evidently a devoted scientist & mountaineer – a man like Browning's Grammarian. I thought of him as a man I was certain to like & get on with when we were thrown together, and I'm sure he is a great loss.

Raeburn is sick at present. He is a weak man I fear & Wollaston has taken him to a haven in Sikhim, where he is to spend a fortnight or so & when he is quite fit rejoin us. He is too old for this job – 55 – & I fear he won't go far anyway. So that Bullock & I are left as the sole climbing experts & neither of us knows anything of the Himalaya. It is a very weak climbing party on the face of it and we shall have to go slowly & cautiously. But on the other hand we shall have a very stout man in Morshead who will be able to climb with us regularly in a later stage; & Howard Bury himself may turn out to be a useful mountaineer.

I hope this letter will go out to-morrow. Our letters came by ordinary postal arrangements to Phari, which is on the route to Lhasa, & from there the English mail is to come on about once a week by a special messenger, who will also take letters back. He is expected to catch us up to-day.

I haven't yet said how continually I was reminded of you in Sikhim – by the datura, which grows very freely there & was in full bloom as we passed through & deliciously fragrant at nights. The trees were not much taller as a rule than your Hobcroft plant, but very wide spread.

I expect some of this news in a repetition of what Ruth will have sent on to you, but it seems much more satisfactory to have written direct – will you please circulate this letter through the family after you & mother have done with it?

Much love to Mother & to you all.
Your loving son,
George

An afterthought.

I suppose this may reach you about July 20, so I must take this opportunity of wishing you many happy returns of July 26 & the same to Trafford of July 11.

Mount Everest Expedition

1st Advanced Camp
July 7, 1921

My dear Mother,

I received your letter dated May 19 yesterday; it was a great
pleasure to hear from you; letters are very rare here, though
now we are more or less stationary. I hope to get a mail at
more or less regular intervals of a week. I'm sorry to say the
supply of ink has run out for the moment, but I hope my
pencil scrawl will survive.

I presume that Ruth is passing on my news in some
fashion, & you will have heard of our trekking from Kampa
Dzong to Tingri. I confess to being rather tired of Tibet &
Tibetans before we reached that destination. The country
indeed has its moments when the form & folds of the bare
hills are softened in the evening light; it can be singularly
beautiful in its fashion; even the bizarre contrast between
flat plains & abrupt snow mountains can be beautiful; a river
with its fertile borders meandering through the desert; a
fresh valley or plain revealed in the day's march, or the
vision from some high ground of endless ranges of hills;
the ruins & the strange monuments – all these affect the
imagination. But the people after one has once observed
their prevailing facial characteristics & costume present
themselves chiefly as superstitious & dirty.

My chief interest since we left the flowers & reached the high lands has naturally been in Mount Everest. Bullock & I made several excursions en route, ascents of commanding hills, by way of reconnaissance, & some of these views were very informing, so that we had a useful general idea of the lie of the country & the shape of the mountain before we reached Tingri.

But it is a very different story now. Here we are in the heart of the mountain country with all its complexity waiting to be resolved. Everest is due south of us. From our camp perched on a shelf under a stony hillside we look straight up the flat narrow glacier to its gigantic northern precipice 7 or 8 miles away. It is incredibly big. The summit is between nine & ten thousand feet above the deep cwms – a rock peak plastered with snow, no airy spire, rather a blunted top built on a great arête, a strong head on broad shoulders. It is a terribly formidable mountain; the faces are appallingly steep; sometimes it seems an impossible idea that anyone should ever reach the summit.

The immediate purpose of our reconnaissance is twofold. We have first to make out the immediate environs of Everest – the approaches; so far we have determined pretty well the approach to the great cwms ahead of us. I was up there a few days ago, but it remains to determine whether a col between Everest & a peak immediately to the N. can be reached from this side & though I have the spot in my eye I haven't actually investigated the camping ground from

which an advance could be made either in that direction or
up the great N.W. buttress which bounds the cwm on the
W. & is a possible line of attack.

Our next object is to penetrate into another cwm which
undoubtedly exists though we haven't seen the bed of it on
the far side of this N.W. arête, enclosed between it & the
high wall of the W. arête. To-morrow we shall set out with
2 light tents, turn to the W up a tributary glacier & encamp
on the moraine at the foot of a small isolated peak standing
curiously in the middle of the great glacier coming down
from this other cwm – or so we think; probably we shall
spend 3 nights there reconnoitering all that side – & then
back to this comparatively civilised spot, where we have at
least a 'bearer' who cooks for us & waits for us, besides some
shelter from the wind on the banks of a tiny lake. And
secondly we shall have to rub our noses against the steep
slopes themselves.

I hope this may give you some idea of the kind of life I'm
leading. Of course a primary object at present is to train our
coolies. They are a fine lot of men but strange to the craft of
mountaineering. Much time is spent in trying to converse
with them in Hindustani, a tongue with which I am still
very ill acquainted; and there are continued difficulties
about arranging supplies from our base camp, a $3^{1}/_{2}$ hrs walk
from here. You know of course that Raeburn is not with us.
He suffered badly from diarrhoea & went down into
Sikhim to recover. I don't expect he will get better enough

for this kind of work though he may get up later to give us the benefit of his advice.

Morshead is still busy with his survey N.W. of Tingri – I hope he will join us towards the end of this month – so that Bullock & I are the climbing party. We badly need a third & Morshead who is evidently a very sturdy man should prove very useful.

I confess to being not altogether displeased at having the management of affairs entirely in my own hands – it is completely my enterprise now & will be so to the end of the chapter – & such an enterprise!

You know there's something of that spirit in my composition, so the confession won't surprise you.

Bullock & I are fairly pleased with ourselves so far. Both of us, he especially, felt the height very much to start with & the sort of fatigue one experiences up here is devastating; but two days ago, and a week after establishing this camp we ascended a peak about 23,500 ft, which must very nearly equal Longstaff's record – I don't much mind about that – the great thing is that from 18,000 ft here we could at so early a stage do so much in the day; it is a very happy omen and we are both as fit as can be. We propose to call our peak Mount Kellas; so far as I know no peak or glacier is named after him though he was so ardent a climber in the Himalaya & I think this will be a fitting way of showing our respect.

Mother, this is going to be a long job & I am a little home-sick. So much still lies in front before we can turn our faces homewards. And then a voyage intervenes. I'm exhilarated by the doing of all this but I'm not sure I was made for such a long time of it. I don't anticipate danger; but it's a very very big job of its kind & every day when I see Everest I am rather appalled. And I don't like being separated from my roots; if it's a long separation for me isn't it longer for Ruth – in spite of all her energy in running the home?

Well, well, we don't make omelettes without breaking eggs. This will turn out a big omelette in my life; let's hope it will be 'cuit à point'. Perhaps the sound of the rain outside has depressed me a little to-night. Why isn't it snowing? We had 3 or 4 inches on the ground this morning.

Now I must lay me down & take the good rest God gives so bountifully. We shall start at sunrise.

Good night to you both.
Your loving son,
George

Mount Everest Expedition

Base Camp, Kharta
August 26, 1921

My dear Mother,

It is a long time since I wrote to you & it requires some
optimism to do so even now. We have received no letters for
4 weeks & my last from England were dated about June 12.
We guess we are cut off by floods in Tibet north of us; the
river here (the Arun) has risen about 30 ft in its gorge & one
of its tributaries swept away a bridge a few days ago –
incidentally one that we shall want to cross on our way
home. However we hopefully sent off some coolies with
letters a week ago & shall be sending some more a few days
hence – with little prospect of hearing what becomes of
them before we start on our homewards march – so
perhaps this may reach you some day.

Bullock & I have finished out reconnaissance. It has been
extraordinarily interesting & even exciting. We started from
here on Aug. 2 with the main object of finding a way to
what we call the 'North Col' which lies between Everest &
the 1st peak on its great north ridge; from this point lies the
only possible way up the mountain. From all we had seen
before both from a distance & from high views to the N.W.
of the mountain when we were on that side we imagined
that a valley must lead directly from here to the North Col

& its water come into the big glacier stream which joins the Arun just below us. In two days march we hoped to have the col in sight & in 3 days perhaps, with favourable weather we should have determined whether it could be approached from this side.

As it was we were taken by a local guide to Chomolungma as they call Everest. In three days after travelling in cloud or with no further prospect than what we could see within a radius of a few hundred yards we made our way to the great valley which lies north of the Makalu–Everest chain.

Aug. 5: On the fourth we woke to see the gigantic East face of Everest at the head of the valley and all the great cirque of mountains to the southeast with their appalling precipices clearing in the mist. Now one of the great ridges of Everest runs almost due N.E. & we were south of it, the valley we were seeking to the north. Could we get round the foot of this ridge & into our valley? Local wisdom said yes & we half believed our guide. It took a day's reconnaissance to dispel the illusion. We found the N.E. edge had no foot. It came down like the N.N.W. to a col from which a great spur was seen to run northward & then turn back to a series of peaks to the east & north of the valley we were camping in.

It was all very puzzling & for all we could see there was no valley going directly to the north col. That point must be definitely settled, so we decided to climb a lovely snow peak, the third from the N.E. ridge of Everest in the very heart of all this complicated country.

Aug 6: A camp was pushed up & we climbed our peak next day, with no small labour.

Aug 7: We looked down upon a great glacier stretching away to the east, the next valley to the north of our camp & we saw its head, a snow col: but this was not the 'North Col' but two miles further east. Between it & the north col lay a whole steep face of Everest & below the face presumably a glacier in a cwm. And where was the exit of this presumed glacier? If not to the east could it be to the north; or even possibly over the North Col itself. Somewhere a valley must exist. How were we to find our way into it?

Aug 8: The following day we went down. I was unwell (tonsilitis I think) & miserable & we learned as we went down that Howard Bury had come up to our lower camp, so it was an obvious plan to stay there for the day on the lovely pastures with the yaks grazing all around us & milk & butter purchasable in plenty – but the [illegible] plan was also obvious; we must retrace our steps; for we had left the big glacier stream we were intending to follow after the first day's march; we must go back to that stream & trace it upwards, & so find our valley.

The Leigh-Mallory family home, The Manor House, Mobberley, in 1865. The boy front left is George's father Herbert, aged 9, who was the youngest of ten children.

George's parents, the Reverend Herbert and Annie Leigh-Mallory (née Jebb), when she was aged 18.

George Leigh-Mallory while at Winchester College, at the ages of 13 and 17.

one can sit & it is as smooth
& comfortable to sit in as a
bath & the water comes
up to the middle of one's chest.
It is so absolutely glorious
here that I cannot find
words to express it, so George
is going to have a turn at the pencil.
Trafford really wants to have what
he calls a 'bed rehearsal'. And oh what
beds! Some feet of hay covered with
blankets - no mattress can beat
that. If Mary & Avie will come (we
intend to stay indefinitely) we can
partition the hut. Or we could
probably find rooms for them in some

'Thank you for sending the <u>silver</u> spoons & forks': a joint letter home penned by a happy George and younger brother Trafford from one of their climbing trips to Snowdonia in August 1908. As they were sleeping in a cow barn, their mother's expensive cutlery may have been redundant. *See page 27.*

George, the young Charterhouse teacher, aged 26, and brother Trafford, aged 19, about to set off from the family home on bicycles for another climbing trip to North Wales, Easter 1912, carrying their ropes and blankets.

A day in the garden with friends: George (*standing, right*) with sister Avie (*seated, middle*), and close friend from Cambridge Geoffrey Keynes (*seated, left*), the brother of renowned economist John Maynard Keynes.

George's elder sister Mary Brooke, née Leigh-Mallory, who he was close to. (Courtesy of Angela Gresham Cooke)

George the Cambridge student and elder sister Mary, picnicking on the River Dee near Chester.

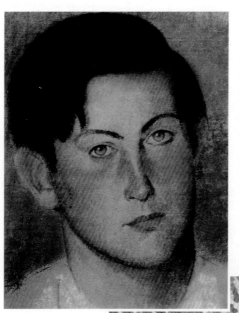

George, by the Bloomsbury Group painter Simon Bussy, *circa* 1910. The young climber's looks and athletic physique made him a popular model among the Bohemian circle. The work now hangs in London's National Portrait Gallery. (Pictures Now / Alamy Stock Photo)

George, bare-chested, painted by the Post-Impressionist Duncan Grant in 1912. Grant – who was Vanessa Bell's lover – used to stay with George for weekends while he taught at Charterhouse. (Celestine Dagli / Alamy Stock Photo)

A naked George, photographed by the Bloomsbury Group artist Vanessa Bell in 1912. George was linked romantically to several members of the group, both male and female. (© Vanessa Bell / Tate)

Ruth Mallory (née Turner), the daughter of the Arts and Crafts architect Hugh Thackeray Turner. George and Ruth met at a dinner party in 1913 when she was 21, and married in July the following year, the day after the outbreak of the First World War. (The Picture Art Collection / Alamy Stock Photo)

'She's brave and true and sweet': George's breathless letter to his mother on May 1st, 1914 revealed not only that he was engaged, but that it was to a woman she had never met. *See page 45.*

See page 45.

CHARTERHOUSE,
GODALMING.

May 1. 1914

My dear Mother

I'm engaged to be married. What bliss! & what a revolution! Ruth Turner — she lives just over the river from here in a lovely house & with lovely people ; — she's as good as gold & brave & true & sweet. What more can I say ! I fixed it up this morning. It was with Ruth & her family that I was staying in Venice & it was these

my own mind became resolved.

When are you coming here & you have never said.

Yr. Lvg son

George

George and Ruth, on the porch of their first marital home, The Holt in Godalming. The gothic spires of Charterhouse School where George taught are visible behind him. The pictures were taken by a friend, the academic Francis Fortescue Urquhart, while he was staying with the couple over a weekend in July 1915, a year after they married.

(Reproduced by kind permission of the Master and Fellows of Balliol College)

Ruth and George, in his Royal Garrison Artillery officer's uniform. George survived 18 months of service on the Western Front and celebrated Armistice Day on November 11th, 1918 with his pilot brother Trafford close to the frontline. (© The Family of Clare Mallory Millikan)

George's letters home from the front, like every other soldier's, were censored and stamped as 'passed' if they didn't contain secrets.

George with his first child, daughter Clare, aged 2, at home while on leave from the Western Front in 1917. He was besotted with his children. Another daughter, Berry, followed that year, and then a son, John, in 1920. (Prismatic Pictures / Bridgeman Images)

George's two loves in life were Ruth and their family, and the mountains. The latter began first, as a schoolboy at Winchester College, when a master took him on a summer trip to the Alps. He developed his own unique climbing style, as graceful as it was swift. George is photographed here on a later trip to the French Alps by his close friend, the mountaineer Geoffrey Winthrop Young. (GRANGER – Historical Picture Archive / Alamy Stock Photo)

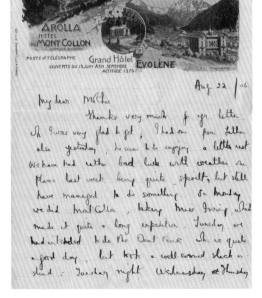

AROLLA
HOTEL
DU MONT COLLON
ALTITUDE 2000M.
POSTE et TÉLÉGRAPHE
Grand Hôtel EVOLÈNE
OUVERTS DU 15 JUIN AU 1ER SEPTEMBRE
ALTITUDE 1375 M

Aug. 22 / 06.

My dear Mother

Thanks very much for yr letter which I was very glad to get; I had one from father also yesterday, he seems to be enjoying a little rest. We have had rather bad luck with weather our plans last week being quite spoilt, but still have managed to do something. On Monday we did Mont Collon, taking Miss Irving, which made it quite a long expedition. Tuesday we had intended to do the Dent Perroc which is quite a good day, but took a well earned slack in stead. Tuesday night Wednesday & Thursday

George's letters home from the Alps contained rapturous descriptions of his climbs. In this one, the 20-year-old Cambridge student writes, after a dawn ascent of the Dent Blanche, how it was 'too inexpressibly glorious to see peak after peak touched with the pink glow of its first sun, which slowly spread until the whole top was a flaming fire, against a sky with varied tints of leaden blue'. See page 24.

'They looked like a Connemara picnic trapped in a snowstorm': the 1921 British expedition to Mount Everest. Standing, from left: A.F.R. Wollaston, expedition leader Charles Howard-Bury, Alexander Heron, lead climber Harold Raeburn. Seated, from left: George Mallory, Oliver Wheeler, Guy Bullock and Henry Morshead. By the time this photograph was taken at base camp, a ninth member, Dr Alexander Kellas, was dead. (GRANGER – Historical Picture Archive / Alamy Stock Photo)

The 1922 expedition. First row, from left: George Mallory, George Finch, Dr Tom Longstaff, expedition leader Brigadier General Charles Bruce, Edward Strutt, Colin Crawford. Second row, from left: Henry Morshead, Geoffrey Bruce, Arthur Wakefield, Howard Somervell, John Morris, Edward Norton. 'I write on the eve of the great adventure,' George told his mother on arrival. (GRANGER – Historical Picture Archive / Alamy Stock Photo)

Members of the 1922 expedition during their trek through the Tibetan plains, practising how to use oxygen tanks. Oxygen was used for the first time that year by George Finch in his summit attempt. Finch set a new height record of 27,300 feet, converting George and others to the benefits of what their local porters nicknamed 'English air'. (J.B. Noel / Royal Geographical Society via Getty Images)

George, third from left, and his team of porters during a rest stop between two camps on Everest in 1922. All three expeditions relied heavily on the tough local mountain men to lug huge loads of equipment to the highest camp possible. (J.B. Noel / Royal Geographical Society via Getty Images)

A photo taken by George himself in 1922, approaching Camp III, looking down the East Rongbuk glacier.

'Now that the prospect revives, I want to have a part in the finish': members of
the 1924 expedition. Back row, left to right: Andrew 'Sandy' Irvine, George with a
playful boot on a friend's shoulder, John de Vars Hazard, Noel Odell and expedition
doctor, R.W.G. Hingston. Front row, left to right: Edward Shebbeare, Geoffrey
Bruce, Howard Somervell and Bentley Beetham. George was the only person to go
on all three expeditions and agonised about returning in 1924. (J.B. Noel / Royal Geographical
Society via Getty Images. Photo was colourised later.)

Base Camp,
Rongbuk
May. 2. 1924

My dear Mary,

It seems ages ago since I received your letter & two postcards. All that you told me about the monsoon was of great interest. This seems the most extraordinary season compared with previous experience of Tibet. The atmosphere has been just as it is during the monsoon & much warmer than in '22; we have to prepare for an early monsoon though I daresay these conditions may not tend to delay it. At present the mountain is very windy, & sprinkled with fresh snow + looks most unpleasant for climbing; it has been quite cold besides up here these last days. I look forward to your next news — but the mail seems to be delayed for ever. I can't tell you how full of hope I am this year. It is all so different from '22 when one was always subconsciously dissatisfied because we had no proper plan of climbing the mountain. And this year it has been a chief object with Norton & me to organise the whole show as it should be organised (sorry the ink has begun to freeze)

George's letter to his sister Mary from Base Camp on May 2nd, 1924. It was so cold that he was forced to switch to pencil – 'sorry the ink has begun to freeze', George told her. The expedition that year suffered from particularly cold and bitter weather. Temperatures on Everest plummeted to a punishing -29°C, freezing George's boots. *See page 173.*

Expedition members and porters in 1924 begin their climb up the North Col. All their supplies had to be lugged up it, a feat George supervised. To his frustration, it took almost all of May because of the appalling weather, pushing the expedition behind schedule. (T.H. Somervell / Royal Geographical Society via Getty Images)

The peaks that surround Everest, photographed at 28,000 feet by Howard Somervell during his summit assault with Teddy Norton in June 1924. It was the highest point on the earth from which a photograph had been taken. Somervell described the sight as 'a perfect sea of fine peaks, all giants among mountains, all as dwarfs below us. The view, indeed, was indescribable, and one simply seemed to be above everything in the world.' (SuperStock / Alamy Stock Photo)

The last photograph: George and Sandy Irvine leaving Camp IV for their final summit attempt, just before 9am on June 6th, 1924. It was a crystal-clear day, and they had their oxygen tanks and masks already strapped on as they made their last checks. (Noel E. Odell / Royal Geographical Society via Getty Images)

'No trace can be found': Noel Odell and two porters lay out sleeping bags in the shape of a cross – the signal for the rest of the expedition watching anxiously below that George and Irvine were missing, presumed dead. The shocking moment was captured on a telephoto lens by the 1924 expedition's cameraman, John Noel.

(J.B. Noel / Royal Geographical Society via Getty Images)

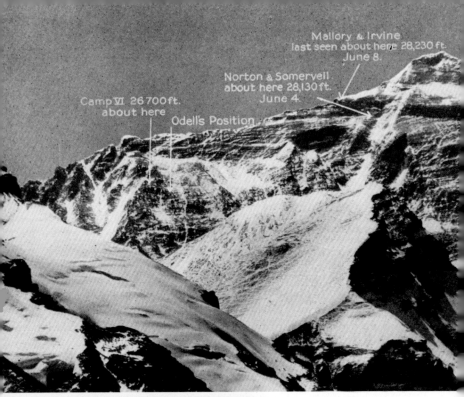

Camp VI 26 700ft.
about here

Odell's Position

Norton & Somervell
about here 28,130 ft.
June 4.

Mallory & Irvine
last seen about here 28,230 ft.
June 8.

IN MEMORY OF
GEORGE HIGH·MALLORY
& ANDREW IRVINE
LAST SEEN 8th JUNE 1924
AND ALL THOSE WHO DIED
DURING THE PIONEER
BRITISH MT. EVEREST EXPEDITIONS

IN MEMORIAM
GEORGE MALLORY
1924

Mount Everest, with the key positions of the 1924 expedition's final days annotated on the North-East ridge. Noel Odell was just below Camp VI when he spotted George and Irvine 'going strong for the top'. He estimated they were just 800 feet from the summit. Published in *The Sphere* in 1924.

(Chroma Collection / Alamy Stock Photo)

The modern memorial erected for George Mallory and Sandy Irvine at base camp on the Tibetan side of Mount Everest, where their climbs began. Alongside it, the stone slab left for George by fellow 1924 expedition members, who also built a stone cairn for the lost pair before leaving for home. The first three expeditions to climb Mount Everest in the early 1920s claimed a total of 13 lives. Since then, more than 320 more people have died on the mountain.

(StockShot / Alamy Stock Photo)

Aug 11: Three days later we established a new mountain base camp. To tell my story in detail would take me too many pages – how I was still unwell & bitterly too disappointed to be missing as it seemed the final act of reconnaissance while Bullock went on alone; how Morshead joined me & Bullock found nothing & the 3 of us went on & after establishing 2 more advanced camps in the thickest of weather eventually made our way to the snow col we had seen on Aug 7. This was by far the finest expedition we have made if one judges by the efforts required. It was a fearful grind in snowshoes over soft snow from 3.0 a.m. to 12.30 p.m. The heat was literally like that of a furnace burning one through the thin haze & eating one's vitality; up the steep final slopes we struggled step by step – & finally saw what we wanted to see, an easy way from this col to the 'North Col' of our desire.

Aug 18: In the photo which I enclose you will see the North Peak appearing over our col & through a magnifying glass you will be able to make out quite a lot of detail. This is the way to Everest & once the snow is hard it will be an easy way to the mountain & to a height of about 23,500 ft. After that we shall see. Meanwhile we must wait for the weather. It is no use attempting to get laden coolies across the snow at present. But the monsoon is supposed to break at the beginning of September – I hope it may. Our stages from Kharta are 2 days for coolies (or 1 for unladen sahibs) to our mountain base camp at 17,500 ft, 1 day thence up a stony

valley to 1st advanced camp above a glacier at 19,900 ft,
1 day to 2nd advanced camp at or near our snow col
22,750 ft, 1 day to the North Col about 23,500, 1 day to
final camp not lower I hope than 26,000 ft under the great
N.E. shoulder of Everest, & 1 day to the summit. Man
proposes . . .

Meanwhile the climate of Kharta is like the softest of
England summer weather; the meadows are green and
starred with blue gentians – I spend much time in
photography, experimenting, developing; printing & much
in simply imagining the journey home & home at the
end of it.

The future is indeed very vague. Much seems to depend on
climbing this great mountain. But in any case I can see
myself lecturing a good deal about Everest this winter – &
so earning some money. There will be no one else to tell the
mountain story as Bullock won't be free & anyway
wouldn't want to.

I wonder, I wonder . . . shall we get up? I think of it &
think & can't see it's impossible – or not for me at all events;
but there's the rub; Bullock is not so strong as I am &
Morshead hasn't the lungs; Wheeler may come to 26,000
but he is troubled by his stomach; the coolies all seem to feel
the height more than we do. And perhaps in the end I shall
give out first – who knows?

Whatever the end, it's been a good adventure so far; and I don't mean the end to be a tame one – if only we have the weather.

Well now Good Night, Mother.

Much love to you both. Will you be at the Mount Everest show in the Queen's Hall on Dec 20? I know no details.

Ever your loving son,
George

Approaching Marseilles
November 11, 1921

My dear Mother,

We came down from Everest on Sept. 25 & I've been
travelling homewards ever since – with only a small
delay, four days in Darjeeling & a little sightseeing in
India on the way through – so that though it's so long
ago, a very, very long time it seems looking back, I've
actually only missed one mail before writing to you. I was
too disappointed to write at first, I think. I tried to
describe it in a long story but somehow it all seemed
unreal & I stopped. But the real disappointment was not
in what we failed to do. The party lost heart in the end –
the causes mainly physical; there was no appetite left for
the adventure; the spirit was dead. That was the tragedy.
It made no difference. We could have done no more & the
vision I carried away of the blown snow endlessly swept
over the grey grim slopes left no room for regrets about the
achievement. But I feel a little sorry for you; there would
have been so much more to blow a trumpet about had we
got a bit higher. It's a very harmless & pleasant amusement
blowing a trumpet. Anyway it's a good story in all & I
shall have lots to tell you about it; & something also
wherewith to satisfy the great British Public, & if it
wants to hear I shall make a little money & gain some
time for writing.

I've had a strenuous time on board ship writing my
report for the Committee – I set myself down the day
after embarking at Bombay & wrote straight ahead, 80
to 90 pages, quite a solid work. One of these days you
must see it.

You know I expect that Ruth is to join me at Marseilles,
actually to-morrow; she's rushing along at this moment
over the plains of France to meet me; & the ship plods on
against the head-wind taking me to her. She won't find me
bald or grey-haired or greatly wrinkled or even
particularly bronzed – just healthy & happy as usual as
though life had been uneventful – or perhaps a bit happier
and gayer. I don't know what her plans may be. She may
have forgotten to make any. I fear the Rhone may be cold &
we shall flee before the Mistral – perhaps westwards &
eventually to Bordeaux; & home I expect one of the first
days in December. I shan't be sorry to get there however
good the South of France may prove. Those dear infants – I
want to see them again too; and all of you for that matter.

Well, I must finish my packing & go to bed.

Much love to you both
Your loving son,
George

6

THE SECOND EXPEDITION (1922)

The Mount Everest Committee tried to persuade George to sign up to the second expedition before the steamship returning him from the first one had even reached England. It was due to depart for Tibet in March 1922, to give the climbers as long as possible on the mountain before the onset of the monsoon. Knowing his value to it, George initially played hard to get. He wanted to secure a promise for more climbers and better resources, and he was successful. The budget for the new expedition was almost doubled to £11,000. It was to have 13 members and a contingent of seven climbers, rather than four. Along with better tents, oxygen tanks were to be taken for the first time.

Only two members from the first expedition returned on the second: George, and the surveyor and mountaineer Henry Morshead, another Old Wykehamist. The new group was also a lot younger, with only one member over 50.

Crucially, it was also under new leadership – that of 56-year-old Brigadier General Charles Bruce.

Unlike the first expedition's leader Charles Howard-Bury, who George and the other climbers had clashed with, Bruce was a bear of a man, cheery and universally popular. He'd also seen the worst of the fighting during the war, suffering severe leg injuries in Gallipoli.

The downside was the turnaround time. It was far quicker than George liked. His much-looked-forward-to reunion with Ruth and the children was short because he'd also agreed to a profitable Britain-wide tour of 30 lectures about the first expedition. This, after all, was his new career.

The expedition members and George sailed together this time on March 2nd and reached Everest in May. As they set up base camp and planned their summit assault, George was brimming with hope, telling his mother: 'I write, so to speak, on the eve of the great adventure.' Howard Somervell, an army surgeon who had dealt with the full horrors of the Battle of the Somme, had taken Bullock's place as his closest climbing buddy. He was 'an excellent companion', George said, even if he didn't quite share competitive George's resilience to altitude. George never voluntarily described anyone as better than him, and perhaps they weren't.

The key to success, the climbers thought, was to establish the highest camp possible as a springboard for the summit. Supplies had to be lugged onto the North Col and then up to at least 25,000 feet – and that could only be done with the help of porters. Their new team of hard-working and hugely resilient local mountain men were again handpicked.

The first attempt was made by Mallory, Somervell, Morshead and Teddy Norton – another new climber and army officer on the 1922 expedition – and aided by nine porters. They set out on May 19th and climbed without oxygen.

It was virgin territory after the North Col, and extremely hard work. Each and every step had to be cut by hand as the surface was rock-hard ice. The cold was bitter, and on reaching 25,000 feet and establishing Camp V, the climbers despatched their shivering and exhausted porters back down the mountain. Fresh snow began falling, making the work even harder. There was a very close shave when several of the party, attached to each other by rope, slipped and started tumbling down the mountain. Their lives were saved by George who instinctively dug in with his ice axe and wrapped the rope around it. At 26,800 feet, exhausted and dehydrated, the party decided they could not go on. They had, however, set a new world record for altitude reached.

George and Norton were ruled out of the second attempt because of painful frostbite to their ears and fingers; the latter were so bad there was a risk of losing some digits altogether. It was with some discomfort that George told his mother that a rival climber on the expedition – the Australian George Finch, who he got on less well with – now stood the best chance of being the first to the top.

Finch was the first to make a summit attempt with the help of oxygen. He climbed notably faster with it and set a new altitude record of 27,300 feet, yet Finch's attempt also had to be abandoned, because of high wind and an oxygen tank malfunction.

The third and final attempt of the expedition was made by George, Somervell and Colin 'Ferdie' Crawford – an accomplished mountaineer and civil servant in India. A party of 17 in total with their porters, they set off from base camp on June 3rd. It ended in terrible disaster.

At 1.30pm on June 7th, just as the party were making the final ascent to the top of the North Col, they were hit by a sudden avalanche, caused by a fresh snowfall. It partially buried George and the other Englishmen, and swept nine porters below them over a 60-foot ice cliff into a crevasse. The desperate party managed to dig out two of the porters alive, but seven were killed.

George was distraught and squarely blamed himself as the leader on the day. He told his mother he should have known more about the condition of the snow. 'It is a terrible blow to me. They were splendid fellows,' he wrote. 'There is no obligation I more earnestly wanted to observe than that of keeping them safe.' He added: 'The General has been as kind as possible & I try not to go around with a face of tragedy [. . .] but such things can't easily be put aside, nor I feel ought they to be. What is done can't be undone, and the worst of this case is that nothing can be done to make good.'

The dead porters' colleagues refused George's offer to dig them out and carry their bodies down, preferring a mountaineer's burial for them instead, so they were left where they fell. The lost seven porters were the first deaths on Mount Everest itself and took the first two expeditions' cumulative death toll to eight. The tragedy ended the 1922 expedition, and in late August George arrived back home.

And yet, everyone – including George – knew they would have to go back again.

Darjeeling
March 22, 1922

My dear Mother,

By the time you get this you will be very near Easter &
your birthday, & I wish you many happy returns. I
wonder when last your birthday fell on Easter Day – I
should have put it the other way round – ; it can't happen
often.

We are having rather longer here than I expected – we
arrived on the 20th & start on the 26th – and I am
staying very happily with the Morsheads. It was good
to find ourselves here after the journey across India.
The hot weather they say, is beginning early this year, &
though it was still bearable in the plains the dust
silting into the railway carriages & covering everything
was most disagreeable. Everything is done to make
travelling comfortable – on the mail train we found even
a bath; & we were served with excellent meals but even
so to be overwhelmed with dust on dust in all one's
quarters as Pharaoh found lice, for 43 hours is quite
enough.

However, I must say that our journey altogether from
London to Darjeeling was vastly more pleasant than my
lonely trip last year besides being so much shorter. We all
got on well together & enjoyed the voyage.

General Bruce is full of activities here & any amount of stuff has already gone on. We shall be travelling in two parties again most of the way to Phari – Bruce, Wakefield, Strutt, Longstaff, Noel (I hope) & self the first party.

It is glorious weather here & we should have a lovely journey through Sikhim. The winter has been rather exceptionally dry which is all to the good, & many flowers are out already, more especially magnolias blooming magnificently near here on the hillsides – you may remember we were too late for them last year. I'm glad to say that Morshead is coming with us. Heron may possibly come too.

I must send this for the post now. Farewell. Much love to you both.

Your loving son,
George

No. 3 Camp
May 15, 1922

My dear Mother,

I must write you a brief note, though I hope you will be
getting my news from Ruth & I find no time to write at
length more than once. Thank you for your letter
received last mail & much delayed. It was the London
Mercury I wanted, a monthly – I thought it cost 2/6d
[two shillings and sixpence] & so would come to no more
than a weekly; but never mind; I find too little time to read
what I have with me; there's a whole volume in one of my
suitcases entitled 'Social Psychology' which I haven't yet
opened & for life at these high camps I find Robert Bridges'
anthology 'The Spirit of Man' provides most that I want.

I write, so to speak, on the eve of the great adventure; –
owing to some failures in the transport arrangements
Somervell & I have been pushed up to make certain of
getting as high as we can apart from all else & later I
suppose if all goes well a big attempt will be made with
oxygen. I like this part of the show better than the other.
We shall be camped on the North Col, I hope, in a few
days' time & our first great effort will be to get 3 or 4 loads
carried one stage further on, say to 25,000 ft. If we can do
that I make little doubt we shall give a good account of
ourselves & really put the matter to the test. The mountain
is very cold at present & even down here at 21,000 ft we

have 15 to 20 degrees of frost in our tent soon after the sun has left us – it leaves all too early soon after 3 p.m.

There's too much wind about at present too – though nothing like so bad as last September it was quite disagreeable on the North Col two days ago. Otherwise the mountain is in good condition now – a very black mountain compared with the sugar cake we were accustomed to look at after the monsoon.

Somervell I find an excellent companion & we get on together excellently. We climb pretty evenly too; he feels the height a bit more than I do at present, but that is better than the other way round & I dare say it will be a different story at the next stage. We're both pretty fit now & tend to become more so as we become better acclimatised.

I must stop now as there are many little things to be done in preparation for a party of coolies whom we expect this morning.

Much love to you both,
Your loving son,
George

Mount Everest Expedition
May 28, 1922

My dear Mother,

The runner who takes the telegraphic despatch about our climb must also take a word from me to you though it will be a long time before you receive it.

Two things are uppermost in my mind; – it was a party of perfect comradeship from first to last, & it is a great experience to go through with an adventure like that with the personal relations – a source of joy & strength; and we were marvelously looked after by Providence, or we should have had no tale to tell.

But to reach the top every circumstance must be favourable & that sort of fortune wasn't ours. It is not disappointing to be failed at the first attempt; it is rather distressing not to be able to make another –; and though neither my fingers nor Norton's ear are bad, they are enough to prevent us going up again – at least one would almost certainly lose the injured member next time. So I'm afraid you mustn't expect any better news, so far as I am concerned.

It is not improbable that Finch may get up with the help of oxygen.

I'm very well after all – a little 'stale' still when it comes to walking, but full of life. Poor Morshead is in rather a bad way & seems much run down, but we have quite good hopes that he will not lose his fingers.

The weather is just on the turn here & after piercing us incessantly with bitter winds begins to be a bit warmer. We shall be turning homewards about June 10 I expect & I should be in England comfortably before the end of August.

Many thanks for your letters & for a copy of the London Mercury just received. It looks a very good number.

Very much love to you both,
Your loving son,
George

I expect Ruth will send on some observations about the climb – but I really feel I told most about it in the narrative, which I suppose the Times will have printed.

Everest expedition, Base Camp
June 11, 1922

My dear Father – Mother,

I know when first you read of our accident you must have
been deeply thankful for my escape & for all your sakes at
home I thank God too. You must also be deeply grieved for
the loss of these men. It is a terrible blow to me. They were
splendid fellows, & there is no obligation I more earnestly
wanted to observe than that of keeping them safe.

I won't discuss now the technical question as to how &
why we were deceived by appearances. The event shows
we were wrong & the conclusion must be that we knew
too little about conditions of snow here. I feel myself
terribly to blame. But we were not pushing on in a reckless
spirit; no one of us three (Crawford too is an experienced
mountaineer & a member of the Alpine Club) had an
inkling of danger.

You will have read in Gen. Bruce's report that we who
survived are safely back at the base & about to start back
on the homeward journey. So you will have no further
anxiety about me. My worst frostbitten finger is almost
well, unlike poor Morshead's. I fear he is condemned to
lose the first joint of at least three fingers on his right hand;
he is now on his way back to Darjeeling with Longstaff,
Strutt & Finch.

I hope to be in England before the end of August. Please let Ruth know what your plans are so that we can arrange a meeting. If by chance you are coming south couldn't you come on & spend a few days in Rouen; it is easily got at, not expensive & contains 3 of the finest churches in France; it would be easy for me to arrange to come back that way & I could devise means for Ruth to communicate with me. I could reach Rouen about Aug. 22. It's just a suggestion; I've never been abroad with either of you.

Sometime I must tell you the story of those last days on the mountain & of the avalanche. At present I'm much too grieved for personal reminiscences. The general has been as kind as possible & I try not to go about with a face of tragedy which can do no one any good; but such things can't easily be put aside, nor I feel ought they to be. What is done can't be undone & we may as well realise that it has made a difference; and the worst of this case is that nothing can be done to make good.

Much love to you both,
Your loving son,
George

Kampa Dzong
July 10, 1922

My dear Mother,
Our mails have been so irregular both incoming & going
that I become rather confused as to when I have received
what; but I believe I have to thank you for two letters &
also for a second copy of the London Mercury which I have
been very glad to have.

The last news I had of you was in a letter from Avie largely
about John, but also telling me that father is now a canon. I
am quite delighted by this news; I feel it has been owing
him for so long & that it is a recognition of all the splendid
work he has done. Best congratulations to you both.

You will see from this address that I am well on my way
home & very glad I am to have my head turned in that
direction. The days we spent in the Kharta district had
collecting for an excuse, but we were really pleasure-seeking.
We saw some very beautiful country, the flowers were a
great joy & we collected some new ones, I think: but the
weather was not very bright & in the Karnah Valley we
were generally in cloud. Somervell, Crawford & I have now
broken off from the main body, my object being to save
some days by short cuts while the others intend staying for
a time in the North of Sikhim, where they hope to get some
fine weather. Tibet is a great deal more agreeable at this time
of year than when we came out. The plains are green, &

even the hillsides are not quite bare. The air is soft & it is a wonderfully coloured landscape. We shall be in Sikhim in two days, we hope & in spite of the rains I expect to enjoy those wonderful valleys in midsummer. Somewhere about July 20 I shall arrive, very wet in Darjeeling. I don't at present intend going back across the continent – but I can easily manage to do so if I hear from you, by getting off my ship at Marseilles. The ship will be the Narkunda, the biggest & most recent of the P&O's so I shall be in luck this time.

I shall have a few days in India on the way through & hope at least to see Delhi. It is more agreeable to have a companion for sightseeing in India so that one can look at things while the other keeps off the crowd; but in Delhi I shall probably meet an old pupil, one Heber Percy – do you remember him, a fresh-faced boy who came with me once to North Wales & stayed a night at Birkenhead on the way back? – now a smart cavalry officer.

Much love to you both,
Your loving son,
George

7

THE LAST EXPEDITION (1922–1924)

The more lethal the pursuit of Everest became, the more the British public's fascination grew. George was also gaining global fame. So much so, that on their return, he and the other members of the second expedition were each awarded an honorary Olympic gold medal for 'Alpinisme'. George agreed to take on more lecture tours ever further afield – Ireland late in 1922, and a two-month trip to the United States in early 1923. In Dublin the halls sold out, but in New York they were only half full. As well as journalists there asking him why he'd want to do such a thing as climb Everest, it seemed Americans were less impressed by his failure so far to do so. George returned disappointed and out of pocket. Everest was not yet enough to live on and he still needed a career that could earn him regular money.

He resolved instead to try out a different form of academia. An external history lecturer's position became available at Cambridge, George's alma mater. He leapt at the opportunity and persuaded a competitive board to hire him. Ruth and the children relocated with him.

The couple loved their fledgling new life in Cambridge. After one lazy afternoon's punting on the river with Ruth, George told his mother: 'It seems more like going back than going forward, as though I should have been married as an undergraduate & were repeating experience now in the married state.'

Meanwhile, the Mount Everest Committee was busy planning the next expedition, this one set for 1924. George was asked to sit on the panel that would pick the climbing members. His biggest dilemma was whether to pick himself.

The committee was again very keen for George to go and badgered him to agree. His inclusion was 'of high importance to the success of the enterprise', it argued. George spent the autumn months of 1923 agonising – or at least outwardly to others. He shared the pros and cons with his father. 'It is an awful tug to contemplate going away from here instead of settling down to make a new life here with Ruth.' After so many years of separation during their marriage – many during which Ruth had no idea whether he'd come back alive – he thought he owed it to her not to go. On the flip side, there was one argument more powerful than any of the others. George simply could not bear the thought of someone else using all his hard work to get to the top instead of him. He confessed: '[Ruth and I] have both thought that it would look rather grim to see the others without me engaged in conquering the summit & now that the prospect revives, I want to have a part in the finish.'

In truth, and whether he knew it then or not, George's decision was predestined. His 38th birthday was approaching. This would be his last chance and he knew it, as he could not do this to Ruth again. His wife again gave him her blessing after also agonising over it, and Cambridge gladly authorised a leave of absence. In November George agreed to attempt the ascent of Mount Everest a third time.

On this occasion the committee favoured continuity. George was among six from the 1922 expedition who were going back. They sailed from Liverpool on February 29th, 1924 – a leap year. General Bruce was again put in charge. Because of the physical degradation suffered by so many of 1922's climbers, it was decided to include some younger men in their 20s. One of them was Sandy Irvine, a powerfully built second-year undergraduate at Oxford who had already won a Boat Race blue in his first year. Irvine was also a keen amateur engineer who had ideas for how to improve the expedition's oxygen tanks. George didn't know him and described him in an early letter on board the SS *California* to his sister Mary as 'young and hasn't much to talk about'. But he warmed to Irvine as the journey went on, calling him 'a very nice fellow' with 'a magnificent body for the job' before their arrival in Calcutta.

Mary was also given a job by George. By then living in the Ceylonese capital Colombo, she was asked to tip him off by telegram as soon as the monsoon arrived there. It would hit Tibet three weeks later, and keeping ahead of it was vital for the climb. George also told Mary how much he looked forward to visiting her in Colombo during his journey home.

The climbers planned to follow the same route as in 1922: up the East Rongbuk Glacier to the North Col, then onto the windy North Ridge, and from there onto the Northeast Ridge all the way up to the summit. Also, as they did in 1922, establishing camps and supplies as high as possible was deemed crucial, but this time they planned to lug even more to even higher camps.

The expedition reached base camp at the foot of the Rongbuk Glacier at the start of May to find the winds unusually cold and strong for that time of year. Yet George was still brimming with optimism. 'I can't tell you how full of hope I am this year. It is so different from '22', he wrote to Mary on May 2nd. Switching to pencil after his ink froze, George was as unbashful as ever: 'Now we've really got a plan (my plan incidentally) [...] I somehow feel we're going to get there this time.' He ended the letter with this sober and prophetic thought: 'Whether we get up or not it will be my job to get the party off the mountain in safety, and I'm keen about that part too – no one climber or porter is going to get killed if I can help it.'

George's plan was for two summit assault parties of two, each trying a different technique. He and Irvine would be the first, climbing with oxygen but thereby carrying more weight, then the two veterans Somervell and Norton next without oxygen and with less weight. The other four climbers would wait at lower camps in reserve. There would be seven camps in total. Camp IV was on the North Col and the last, Camp VII, would be at 27,300 feet and within touching distance of the summit. George's choice of Irvine as his partner over the other significantly more experienced mountaineers remains controversial. His explanation in letters home for picking Irvine was because he was 'a tower of strength' and 'a mechanical genius' who knew how to fix the oxygen tanks, should they malfunction, though some historians have since focused on George's physical descriptions of Irvine, making crude allusions to his Bloomsbury days.

As May went on, the weather continued to worsen and temperatures dropped further. One morning, it plummeted to a punishing -29°C, freezing George's boots so that it was a struggle to even put them on. The appalling weather made even reaching the North Col a Herculean task. By now the expedition's lead climber, George had picked an elite team of 55 'tiger porters' to help heave their large load of equipment and supplies up to the ever higher camps with them, but even these supermen began to seriously struggle with altitude sickness, frostbite and exhaustion. The porters began to drop out, and by the middle of the month, there were just 15 of them left. 'It has been a very trying time with everything against us', George told Ruth in a letter that he asked her to circulate around the family. They did finally reach the North Col but were forced to retreat down, recuperate and wait for the weather to turn.

Still George was not deterred, despite the race against time with the arriving monsoon, which could strike any day now. Defeat to him was still unimaginable and he told his mother he was 'fit, strong and happy', adding: 'We are going to succeed.'

When the weather appeared to improve, they tried again. It was just as tough. The physical exhaustion among the Englishmen was now mounting too. They fought a never-ending battle with the wind while having to cut every step they took in the hard ice under their feet, and all in ever thinner air. A very tired George revealed how, on one journey between camps, he misjudged the snow beneath him and plummeted straight into a deep crevasse. Ten feet down a 'very unpleasant black hole', by chance his ice axe wedged against its sides, stopping his fall and saving his life. The climbers had also each developed nasty coughs that 'tear one's guts', George reported, and pounding headaches that made sleep all but impossible. They were again forced to withdraw back to Camp I to recuperate.

The 1924 expedition was failing, just as the previous two had before it. George was down, but still refused to be beaten. 'I look back on tremendous effort and exhaustion and dismal looking out of a tent door into a world of snow and vanishing hopes', he said. 'And yet and yet and yet . . .' For their third push, after much soul searching, the climbers came up with a new approach, 'a simpler quicker plan'. They would leave most of the porters behind and make a mad dash for the summit alone in their pairs, without the heavy oxygen tanks. It was a desperate last throw of the dice.

Ten days before his disappearance, George wrote his last letter home. It was to his mother Annie, and he told her:

> It has been a hard time altogether & depressing – but we remain undepressed. The train is all laid now – we are recuperating [. . .] It will be a great adventure if we get started before the monsoon hits us – with just a bare outside chance of success.

His last words to her were: 'I shall take every care I can you may be sure.'

On May 30th, George began the new assault but with Geoffrey Bruce as his partner – General Bruce's cousin – who was judged to be fitter than Irvine. They made it to 25,200 feet where they pitched Camp V, before having to turn back yet again when their weather-bashed porters refused to go any further. Somervell and Norton went next on June 2nd. Aided by the establishment of George's new camp, they passed through it and pitched Camp VI at 26,800 feet. But their bid also ended in painful failure two days later on June 4th. The men's pace had been reduced to a crawl by the extreme altitude, and they had to stop after every 12 steps to catch their breath. A physically shattered Somervell dropped out first. Racked by coughing fits that were slowly choking him, he eventually hacked up a great lump of flesh. It turned out to be the entire lining of his throat, which was badly frostbitten and had become detached. Norton pressed on alone, but almost certainly now suffering from oxygen deficiency he took off his snow goggles to try to see the difficult terrain better. He was forced to a halt half-blinded, but tantalisingly close, just 900 feet from the summit.

With Norton's solid encouragement, a desperate George decided to give it one final push – this time with Irvine and some oxygen tanks that had made it up to Camp III. Everyone knew that it would be the 1924 expedition's very last chance. It was also George's, as this had to be his very last expedition.

Just before 9am on June 6th, the pair left the North Col. It was a crystal-clear day. Another climber, Noel Odell, took the last photograph of George and Irvine with their oxygen tanks already on their backs and their masks on their faces. By the end of the day, they had made it to Camp V, and were at Camp VI by the end of June 7th.

That evening, George wrote two notes for the party below him, which he despatched down with his final remaining porters. One note told the expedition's photographer John Noel where and when to start looking for them through his long lens the next day. The other apologised for the state in which he and Irvine had left Camp V. He signed off: 'Perfect weather for the job!'

It was George's last ever contact with the world.

London & North Western Railway
Holyhead, Kingstown & Dublin Express Steamers
Royal Mail Route

November 29, 1922

My dear Mother,

Thank you for your letter, I have hugely enjoyed Dublin.
The audience at the Theatre Royal was one of the best I
have had – a big theatre literally full (only 2 seats
unoccupied I was told); only the gallery was open to
the public; the rest of the seats were taken by members of
the Royal Dublin Society & their friends. And I think the
lecture was a real success.

I was staying with Mrs. Green the widow of J.R. Green the
historian, who is a regular old intellectual grande dame, &
saw a lot of people. It was very interesting picking up
threads spun during my visit 2 years ago & hearing all about
that poor country. There is evidently a crisis just at present,
though no incident of importance occurred during the last
two days. People are very much divided in opinion as to the
result of the executions. The most level-headed regard
Childers' execution, or at all events the manner of it, a
mistake having regard to his great services to Ireland; &
there is some fear of increased bitterness & vendetta
resulting. But I cannot help thinking they must make an
example of some rebels if ever they are going to end civil war.

I had no difficulty in getting admittance to the government building in order to see former acquaintances now 2 of them [are] interred as ministers & went twice to the Dáil which is rather too sober & orderly from a spectator's point of view – very interesting nevertheless.

The only sort of danger to a visitor to Dublin is that he might be too near the scene of action in case of an ambush – a very small chance. The surface of life appears normal though little business in going on they say.

Your loving son,
George

31 Jesus Lane
Cambridge

June 24, 1923

My dear Mother,

Thank you very much for the portfolio which reached me safely & found me in the throes of packing in my study. It is a very nice one & will be most useful.

Here we are in a punt on the river – Ruth conducting me under the bridges. It seems more like going back than going forward, as though I should have been married as an undergraduate & were repeating experience now in the married state. The boat is rather unsteady as we have met the muddy bottom opposite Kings.

We are still in uncertainty about a house – but a glorious uncertainty. We have definitely turned down the house we were after – it wasn't good enough for the large figure asked – they wanted £3650 & we should have spent up to £4000 & even then should have wanted to spend more on a structural alteration. And as against that prospect we decided to build. I worried for R. on Thursday morning; she came up the same day & it was all settled with an architect next morning in time to give the answer I had promised for midday Friday. And meanwhile another house had come into the question – one we had always regarded as

too big even to look at – £4800 asked. This turns out to be
a really fine house & so much more worth spending money
to buy that we have made an offer of £4000 & this is being
considered. It really will be an amazing piece of fortune if
we can get this house. It has a good open situation looking
over the Varsity Rugger ground to the South & with a
half-view of Coton beyond the ranges to the West.

To meet the expense of decoration & the high assessment for
rates & taxes we intend if we get it to start anyway with a
P.G or even two during term. And if we don't get it we
shall build on a site just above Trinity Conduit, which you
may remember is on the north side of Madingley Road a
little way beyond the Observatory – rather far out but in
the country & on high ground – comparatively!

Very few people are up at present. We lunched with Arthur
Benson 2 days ago & there are a few old friends about. It is
rather a busy time arranging for the Jubilee Conference local
lectures on July 6–10. I find Birkenhead & L'pool are among
the very oldest centres.

Much love to you both,
Your loving son,
George

17 Carlyle Rd
Cambridge

October 25, 1923

My dear Father,

I must let you know what is going on – read first the
enclosure which explains itself. This is backed up by a reply
from Hinks to a question of mine as to whether Gen. Bruce
is as keen as all that; – 'I think I can say that not only Bruce
but all the members of the Committee are anxious that you
should go. I have never heard any expression except of fear
that the University might not be able to spare you.'

Cranage has taken a view more sympathetic to my going
then I dreamed of expecting – Hinks's application also
being much stronger than I contemplated – & the whole
matter came up yesterday before the Lecture Committee
(beyond which lies the Syndicate which appointed me), &
they were unanimously & cordially of opinion that so far as
my work was concerned they could not resist an application
of that kind, & that I should be given leave of absence – the
final decision of course to rest with the Syndicate.

You'll see that most likely I shall be free to go & it will
therefore rest with me to make the choice.

You may imagine it isn't easy & I look for guidance as to
what is right. I've been taken rather by surprise as Hinks

wrote without consulting me & I had largely assumed that opinion here would go the other way – & so it is an awful tug to contemplate going away from here instead of settling down to make a new life here with Ruth. We have both thought that it would look rather grim to see others without me engaged in conquering the summit & now that the prospect revives I want to have a part in the finish; apart from that, for any fun I may get out of the expedition or réclame I wouldn't look at it for a moment; my preference is all the other way. But I don't think it can really be decided on these sort of grounds at all. Ruth comes in of course; she has written that she is willing I should go & we shall discuss it this weekend. Taking that for granted my present feeling is that I have to look at it from the point of view of loyalty to the expedition & of carrying through a task begun; & there I can't help feeling what the people have felt; Rendell for instance was evidently unhappy about my tying myself up here & I feel that it is generally expected of me to go again if it is possible for me.

These are other points, one of them of real importance, the effect of going upon my career; with regard to that St John Parry, Vice Master of Trinity, chairman of the Lecture Committee is quite clear that my prospects will not be injured.

Well there it all is.

Our furniture is being packed to-day & to-morrow (it's almost to-morrow but not quite) & will travel during the week-end & moved in Monday or Tuesday. R. comes here Saturday, to share the double bed which occupies about the whole of my bedroom; & the children next week.

What are your plans? And which day do Mary & Ralph go off.

Love to you all,
Your loving son,
George

Enclosed with the previous letter to Herbert Leigh-Mallory, transcribed in George's handwriting.

*

October 18, 1923

My dear Cranage,

The Mt Everest Committee are very anxious that Mallory should be a member of the expedition next year & that everything possible should be done by them to assist him in obtaining leave from the University to go on the expedition. As I was partly responsible in the 1st instance etc (my appointment), allow me to say this, that it is of very great importance to the enterprise, if he is willing to go a third time, as I imagine he is, should have as much consideration as possible in regard to leave of absence; and I can only ask you to convey to the proper quarters the assurance that Mallory's co-operation next year is of high importance in the opinion of the Mt Everest Committee to the success of their enterprise. I ask you therefore to take as sympathetic a view as you can.

A.R. Hinks

Rannards
November 7, 1923

My dear Father,

It's all settled & I'm to go again[.] I only hope this is a right
decision. It has been a fearful tug. I've had to think
precisely what I was wanted for. They think I can help to
keep it all safe; I think that too a bit. And then I was
guided a bit by the attitude of the Lecture Committee &
the Syndicate. Both unanimous to give me leave &
favourably disposed to my going – they've granted me half
pay for the six months.

I saw the doctors yesterday. They say I'm absolutely A1,
heart & all perfect.

I hate leaving anxieties behind. But it means a lot that we
now know pretty well all about the risks and how to
manage for the best.

I've just been taking my class here – it is really interesting
work; the previous three years' class had been very slack & I
found no idea of reading or writing papers as being essential
parts of the scheme of education, without which in fact it is
of little use, but I think I have got a start with the reading
now & they seem a keen nice lot of students – mostly
young men & maidens in various walks of life between
teachers & boot-making hands.

It is being a very strenuous time with me altogether with a good many ends to the job which have to be picked up.

I hope you are both keeping fit. It must have been rather a blow losing the Brooke family after they had been with you so long.

Will you please thank Mother very much for the photo. It seems to me a good likeness & I like it very well; I am very pleased to have it. I only opened the packet today.

Our house is getting on – three rooms finished beside the kitchen – it's hard work keeping down extras & we were dismayed to find no hot water in either pantry or scullery – a £16 job or thereabouts to put it in.

Much love to you both,
Your loving,
George.

Anchor Line
T.S.S. *California*
March 1, 1924

My dear Mary,

I had your last letter not so very many days ago & a very good letter it was. Like a good many other answers I put you off to the time of great freedom when I should be on board ship, with three weeks clear ahead before we get to India.

I wonder if you know of these ships, this & her sister, which are occasionally deflected from the Atlantic service to make the eastward trip? They are new ships each almost 17,000 tons I'm told & anyway very superior is this one in the whole manner of its 'get up'. She comes from Glasgow like almost everyone on board, the crew from Captain to cabin boy besides the majority of the passengers – luckily I recall my experiences with the Clyde R.G.A. [Royal Garrison Artillery] and get on quite well with the language.

My three companions, Beetham, Irvine & Hazard are seemingly excellent folk, particularly the first. Hazard with whom I share a room seems a bit stiff. Irvine is young & hasn't much to talk about; he was two years in the Oxford boat & knows a lot about engineering lore – quite one of the best.

A considerable asset on board is a gymnasium where you are able to ride either a camel or a horse besides exercising oneself in more expected ways.

Our cabins are bigger than any I had on the P&O & altogether one is very comfortable. As we have return tickets by the same line it is possible that I may come back from Calcutta – not a pleasant journey during the monsoon & further possible that the ship will call at Colombo; some do & some don't. Even so the only way I can see of getting a good look at you is a possible train journey beating the boat by some few days.

It would be lovely to come and see you in Ceylon on the way back; your description makes me long to see the interior. I suppose it will still be raining fairly hard in mid-July, the most likely time?

You seem to be in luck's way altogether – the club, the car, & most of all your own bungalow. I expect the round, daily ending at the club must be a bit monotonous & you'll find the circle a bit narrow perhaps but by now you will vary proceedings with the car. I wonder if you get any safe bathing?

I was living in rather a whirl at Cambridge up to the last moment; twice a week R. and I would go over to my evening classes at Halstead & Raunds, each about 33 miles away, which meant starting at 4 or not much later and getting back 11 or after. Most weeks I was away for some purpose another night besides; & with that beginning weeks were being filled up extremely tight. However we were seeing a good many nice people, either at our house or going out.

We go on being well pleased with the house; they are nice sunny spacious rooms to live in & look well enough after our efforts, though we made one or two mistakes. The Fives Court has been used quite a lot & I have had some very good games in it. We've not had a great success with winter flowers – the stove is so large that we can't at present afford to burn it except when the weather turns really cold; it heats the lower rooms, the conservatory & greenhouse well enough when we use it, but once or twice we have been caught by frost – it has been an exceptionally cold February after a comparatively mild January.

Trafford & Doris were staying with us not long ago & Avie at the same time. 'The Traffords' have had a hard winter as Mother has probably told you. Doris seemed well enough with us; Tr. was not at his best & had flu afterwards; however they are wonderfully contented folk, much more than we should be living so long in a second rate hotel. Tr. looks forward without a doubt to successes & promotion in the future & is quite sure he is at the heart of Imperial Defence at present; & I daresay he does his job very well. He hopes at a spell at the staff college after another year at the Air Ministry.

Ruth after a rather depressed period has been well – cheerful lately. She has had some little trouble with her back, probably muscular rheumatism. The children have had flu, but mildly & all are well too now; Clare much stronger than she was in the autumn.

It's a tug leaving them all this time, especially as Ruth undoubtedly feels it much more. Father is very glad I'm going again. I don't know where it will be best to post this, probably Bombay, as our transit will be speedy – so I'll leave it open for the present to go & dress for dinner –

March 17;

Here we are nearing the journey's end – we shall reach Bombay to-morrow night & 18 days from Liverpool, which is as fast as any boat coming east I fancy. It has been a good voyage too – a sticky time in the Red Sea with a following wind but only for two days; light breezes & sunny skies have been the rule. After employing myself morning– evening with [a] 'medicine ball' I'm pretty fit. One needs to be, as we shall be leaving Darjeeling on the 26th or 27th I suppose.

Our advance guard may have left already as there was some talk of people going up to Gantza, one march below Phari to get trained & acclimatised before getting up on to the high land of Tibet.

Some time on board has been spent playing about with the oxygen apparatus. Irvine is a great dab at things mechanical

& has some criticisms to make; & there are certainly a good many chances that it will go wrong or break if we use it; we broke one of the high pressure tubes that are supposed to stand any amount of bending putting [it] away into its box today. However I rather expect we shall use it as we can carry 50% more oxygen than last year with the same weight. Norton was keen to go up without oxygen from 26,000, but we've got to camp higher than that to have a chance. Anyway we've got to get up this time & if we wait for it & make full preparations instead of dashing up at the first moment some of us will reach the summit I believe. Anyway it's going to be a good show – a better party than last time I expect though it's impossible to say for certain how anyone will go very high. I wish Irvine had had a season in the Alps. He has a magnificent body for the job. And he's a very nice fellow.

Mind you write to me soon after you get this & I'll write from Phari or earlier; & send me a telegraphic address.

Love to you all
Your affectionate brother,
George

Anchor Line
T.S.S. *California*
March 3, 1924

My dear Mother,

I must post you a line from Gib [Gibraltar] to let you know
how I'm getting on. We are just past Lisbon – seeing quite a
lot of the coast at intervals after passing Finisterre, with a
bright sun, soft fleecy clouds, the air of spring & the sea grey
blue & sparkling. And [the] decks to-day are suddenly
populated, even over-populated, while yesterday as we
rolled across the Bay of Biscay in storm & rain only a few
hardy souls sat about wrapped up in overcoats & rugs.

Luckily we are to drop ¾ of our passenger at Port Said –
they have been gathered by some agency for a tour in
Egypt & we shall have plenty of room when the weather
comes hot. They seem a nice lot of people on board with
not more notable exceptions than one might expect. Of
those bound to Bombay a considerable proportion are
soldiers, among some of whom I find myself at table – quite
nice folk near me. Nothing else matters in comparison.

It was a good thing you decided to depart before seeing us
move off the other day. The two tugs which were supposed
to pull us off never looked like moving us against that
wind & it was 8.30 or thereabouts before we were
underway.

All four of us have survived the sailing – she's a remarkably sturdy ship. Hazard & I get on very happily in our splendid cabin. I occupy the top berth & have the one reading lamp – he fortunately has not the habit of reading in bed.

Well, it was a very good way of leaving England & I enjoyed our sending off very much. It is nice to be seen off in such style.

I find I have a number of letters to write for this first mail & time disappears in a mysterious way, so I'll write no more at present.

Love to you both,
Your loving son,
George

We have a new address this year

Everest Expedition,
c/o British Trade Agent,
Yatung
Tibet

Yatung is two marches below Phari & letters will go straight there I suppose from the rail head in the Teesta Valley without going to Darjeeling. I shall hope to get one mail before we leave Darjeeling – but we don't lose much time – Bombay on the 19th & if we can go on that day Darjeeling on the 22nd. I hope to get 5 days there.

Hotel Mount Everest
Darjeeling
March 25, 1924

My dear Mother,

Many thanks for your letter which reached me to-day on
the eve of our departure. We arrived here punctually. How
curious it is that you heard the California did not leave
L'pool till the morning after you saw me off – she was
delayed only because two tugs were not enough to pull her
out against the wind & when more came to the work we
got off at about 7.30 p.m I think.

The last part of the voyage was very comfortable with
far fewer passenger & plenty of room. We had some
warm days & stuffy nights when our cabins were difficult
to sleep in, but it was a comfortable ship & there were
plenty of corners where one could escape & be quiet. The
journey across India was distinctly hot; it was very dusty
& unpleasant in Bombay the day we landed there & we
had an inferior sort of mail train with old coaches.
However we snoozed a good deal & the nights were
cooler than on the sea though the maximum day
temperature must have been over 100°. I was glad enough
to get to the end of the journey. It is dry & hazy here &
for the first time since we came up we just dimly made
out Kanchenjunga to-day.

The hot weather has evidently begun in good time & that is more likely to mean an early monsoon than a late one, owing to the heating up of the plains of northern India. But there is not a sign of its approach at present – the air is dryer than usual – so we may still hope that it will come late. I have just been writing to Mary asking her to send us news of the weather from Colombo where the monsoon is at least 3 weeks earlier than at Everest & if she sends a telegram as soon as the heavy rain sets in there we should have about 10 days' warning.

I feel it is not only a very strong party this year but a very nice one. Hingston the new doctor is particularly nice. I hear that Shebbeare one of the transport officers is a very good man, he is from the forestry department & knows all about trees & shrubs. We start for Kalimpong early to-morrow morning & there divide, one party going on next day & the other staying a second night; I shall be with the second party this time with Norton, Hingston, Irvine & Shebbeare I believe.

We have had a busy time here & I could have done with a few more days; still I'm pretty fit & prepared to enjoy the journey once more.

Much love to you both,
Your loving son,
George

Hotel Mount Everest
Darjeeling

March 25, 1924

My dear Mary,

It has occurred to me that you can be very useful to us! Of
all things we shall want to know when to expect the
monsoon & we may be able to get an idea as to whether it
is late or early & by how many days if you can supply
information as to what the monsoon is doing in Colombo;
so I want you if you will to do three things.

1. Find out the average date for the beginning of the
   monsoon in Colombo.
2. Write about once in five days a p.c. to say what
   the weather is doing, e.g. 'Heavy cloud, rain
   expected' or 'Clear sky after 3 days intermittent
   rain' or whatever it may be. Dates of course
   required.
3. Send a wire to me at Chomolung, Phari as soon as
   it is <u>absolutely certain</u> that the first heavy rain of
   the monsoon has begun in Ceylon.

And now I have just been talking to Norton who agrees
that this information may be very valuable to us & he
suggests a fourth thing; – sometime, perhaps a week or ten
days after the monsoon begins, it is generally known

whether it is <u>light</u>, <u>heavy</u>, or <u>normal strength</u>; we
ought to know that too; it might make a vital
difference to our plans – so will you also telegraph that
information.

The monsoon must be at least 3 weeks earlier with
you so there should be a considerable margin of time,
as we have a specially speedy postal service arranged
this time, for us to get warning from your pcs [postcards] &
telegrams.

We are having what seems a very short halt here – from
Friday to Wednesday – with a great many things to
be done in it; still it is very nice to be here after the
dusty heat of the plains for 3 days. There's no doubt
travelling in India is an invention of the Evil One – at
all events before the rains. We were just caught by the
heatwave too.

All the party is assembled here but one who is at
Kalimpong. It is really a topping good party this year with
no duds I think. I particularly like our doctor man,
Hingston. Norton is in great form as second in command
arranging things admirably; we're all very fit by the looks
of us.

I have to get my English mail off to-day, so no more now.

Please address – Everest Expedition,

c/o Postmaster,
Darjeeling
& not as I told you.

Love to you all.
Your affectionate brother,
George

Base Camp
Rongbuk

May 2, 1924

My dear Mary,

It seems ages ago since I received your letter & two postcards. All that you told me about the monsoon was of great interest. This seems the most extraordinary season compared with previous experience of Tibet. The atmosphere has been just as it is during the monsoon & much warmer than in '22; we have to prepare for an early monsoon though I daresay these conditions may only tend to delay it. At present the mountain is very windy & sprinkled with fresh snow & looks most unpleasant for climbing; it has been quite cold besides up here these last days. I look forward to your next news – but the mail seems to be delayed forever.

I can't tell you how full of hope I am this year. It is all so different from '22 when one was always subconsciously dissatisfied because we had no proper plan of climbing the mountain. And this year it has been a chief object with Norton & me to organise the whole show as it should be organised (sorry the ink has begun to freeze) & now we've really got a plan (my plan incidentally) which seems to give good chances of success. And here I am at Camp II (I could not get on with this letter at the Base Camp) in the first stages of carrying it out. The first assault on or about May 17 will be with two parties of two, one with & one without oxygen, the respective two being Irvine & myself & Somervell & Norton. The difficult personal questions have all been arranged in the friendliest possible manner. The plan of course had to come first & a most important part of it is leaving an adequate reserve – equal in strength to the vanguard – to make other assaults if the first parties fail. Now the first great difficulty is in establishing the highest camps & for that previous experience is of great importance. It was easily decided therefore that Somervell & I should lead each one of the first two parties. Naturally each wanted to go without oxygen: but on last time's performance it looks as though Somervell after going without gas will be more likely than me to recover for a 2nd attempt; & Norton considers me a more sober & proper companion for Irvine who has had practically no mountaineering experience. He'll be a splendid companion; he is a mechanical genius & a tower of strength & an absolutely sound fellow right through & he'll go well on the mountain & make no rush or silly steps. I somehow feel we're going to get there this time. And I believe Somervell & Norton, who will have two camps about 23,000 against our one have a very fair chance of getting there too. Norton goes with Somervell not altogether because no one is a better goer – I don't feel quite sure about that – but besides being a hard man to beat he'll be immensely useful in getting the porters up to 27,000 – he speaks their lingo & none of the rest of us do except Geoffrey Bruce.

Well then on May 17 the four of us should join up somewhere about the base of the final pyramid – & whether we get up or not it will be my job to get the party off the mountain in safety, & I'm keen about that part too – no one climber or porter is going to get killed if I can help it – that would spoil all.

It is May 4 & I'm in bed, the only tolerable place about 8 p.m. I shan't sleep again under 21,000 until we've had our whack – plenty of time for acclimatisation & meanwhile I shall be seeing through our elaborate bundobust [preparation], counting loads up to the North Col etc.

I can barely see by this single candle lantern. So Good Night.

I've good hope of seeing you if we can get the mountain climbed early.

Much love to you all
Your affectionate brother,
George

I've never all said Thank you for your letter and pcs.

May 16

There's been never a chance all this while of despatching this letter; & meanwhile I've had a letter & p.c. from you,

and before you get this you will have read news of our
reverse. The weather was really impossible & as we must
have our porters fit & happy to do any good when it comes
to the point of attack, the only possible plan was to retreat
& wait. Now the weather looks better – but the first
possible day for reaching the summit is May 28 instead of
May 17 & if the monsoon is early we may get caught. We
shall be going up the glacier again to-morrow – the old gang
once more the vanguard.

I'm afraid the chances of seeing you are disappearing down
the Tibetan wind at this rate. I didn't mean to be later than
about July 9 from Colombo (Ellerman City from Calcutta
advertised July 5) – but I might come down by train & have
a few days with you even now. Will you write to
Darjeeling – Everest Hotel, <u>To await arrival</u> & tell me your
nearest station; if I came across from South India I imagine
if would not be necessary to go all the way down to
Colombo. Also if you can, will you let me know the cost of
1st Class Orient line from Colombo to Marseilles. I have an
unfortunate return by the City line either from Bombay or
Colombo – but I may be able to get rid of it & save time.
Probably delay in getting transport here will settle the
question – but let us still hope to bring off my visit.

Love to you all,
George

To update on his progress while at higher altitudes and to conserve his energy, George would write long, detailed letters in diary form over several days to all his family, care of Ruth, who would type and circulate them. This is one of those letters, and details the immense struggles the climbing parties suffered in the first two weeks of May as they attempted to establish a foothold on the mountain.

*

Base Camp
May 11, 2024

Now I must give you a brief record of the days that have passed since leaving the B.C. [Base Camp]. It has been a very trying time with everything against us. The porters have seemed from the first short of acclimatisation and up against it.

May 3:
Irvine, Odell, Hazard and self to Camp 1. Half the porters lagged badly. Having added a good deal of stuff on their own account to what we had given them to carry they had big loads.

May 4:
I decided to leave 5 loads not urgently required at Camp 1 and have five men to carry all the porters' blankets etc. The N.C.O. (Churka) at 1 was very incompetent in getting

these things distributed. However the result was good and the man must have gone well. Irvine and I had gone ahead and reached Camp 2 at about 12.30; we had hardly finished a leisurely tiffin when the first porters arrived. Camp 2 looked extraordinarily uninviting although already inhabited by an N.C.O. and two others in charge of the stores (150 loads or so) which has already been carried up by Tibetans. A low irregular wall surrounded a rough compound, which I was informed was the place for the Sahibs' tents and another already covered by the fly of a Whymper tent was the home of an N.C.O. The Sahibs' compound was soon put sufficiently in order, two Whymper tents were pitched there for the four of us while a wonderful brown tent of Noel's was pitched for him. No tents were provided here for porters; the intention was to build comfortable huts or 'sangars', as we call them, using the Whymper flys for roofs, but no sangars had yet been built and accommodation for 23 men is not so easily provided in this way. However I soon saw that the ground would allow us to economise walls and Irvine and I with 3 or 4 men began building an oblong sangar, the breadth only about seven feet; other men joined in after resting. It is an extraordinary thing to watch the conversion of men from listlessness to some spirit of enterprise; a very little thing will turn the scale; on this occasion the moving of a huge stone to form one corner started the men's interest and later we sang! And so these rather tired children were persuaded to do something for their comfort, without persuasion they would have done nothing to make life tolerable. Towards

3 p.m. Odell and I (Irvine seemed tired after prodigious building efforts) went to reconnoitre next day's march over the glacier. We began by going along the stones of the true left bank, the way of 1922, but the going was very bad, much more broken than before. To our left on the glacier we could see the stones of a moraine appearing among the great ice pinnacles. We gained this by some amusing climbing, retraced our steps a little way along it towards Camp 2 and then on the far side reached a hump from which the whole glacier could be seen rising to the South; from a point quite near us it was obvious there could be no serious obstacle and that point we saw could be gained in a simple way; it only remained therefore to make a good connection with Camp 2. We followed easily down the moraine which is a stony trough between high fantastic ice pillars and a beautiful place, and just as we were nearing camp found a simple way through the pinnacles, so in an hour and a half the first most difficult part of the way from 2 to 3 had been established.

May 4th to 5th:
An appalling night, very cold, considerable snowfall and a violent wind.

May 5th:
Result: signs of life in camp very late. The first audible one in camps up to and including 2 is the blowing of Yak dung fire with Tibetan bellows.

The men were an extraordinarily long time getting their
food this morning. The N.C.O. seemed unable to get a
move on and generally speaking an Oriental inertia was in
the air. It was with difficulty in fact that the men could be
got out of their tents and then we had further difficulty
about loads; one man, a regular old soldier, having
possessed himself of a conveniently light load, refused to
take a heavier I wanted taken instead; I had to make a great
show of threatening him with my foot in his face before he
would comply and so with much difficulty about it and
about what should be left behind in the way of coolie rations
and blankets and cooking pots, and the degree of illness of
those reported sick, we didn't get fairly away until 11 a.m.

Now making a new track is always a long affair compared
to following an old one, and on this occasion snow had
fallen in the night. The glacier which had looked innocent
enough the evening before was far from innocent now. The
wind had blown the higher surfaces clear. The days, I
suppose, had been too clear for melting and these surfaces
were hard smooth rounded ice, almost as hard as glass and
with never a trace of roughness and between the projecting
lumps lay the new powdery snow. The result of the
conditions was much expenditure of labour either in
making steps in the snow or cutting them in ice and we
reached a place known as 'The Trough', a broken trough in
the ice, 50 feet deep and about one third of the way up,
knowing we should have all that we could do to reach
camp 3. We followed along in the trough some way, a lovely

warm place, and then came out of it into the open glacier where the wind was blowing up the snow maliciously. The wind luckily was at our backs until we rounded the corner of the North Peak, and then we caught it blowing straight at us from the North Col. As the porters were now nearly exhausted and feeling the altitude badly our progress was a bitter experience. I was acting as lone horse finding the best way and consequently arrived first in camp. It was a queer sensation, reviving memories of that scene, with the dud oxygen cylinders piled against the cairn which was built to commemorate the seven porters killed two years ago. The whole place had changed less that I could have believed possible seeing that the glacier is everywhere beneath the stones. My boots were frozen hard on my feet & I know we could do nothing now to make a comfortable camp. I showed the porters where to pitch their tents at 6.30 p.m. got hold of a ruck-sack containing 4 linna cookers, dirked out 3 and meta for their cooking to the porters, and 1 to our own cook; then we pitched our own 2 Meade tents with doors facing about a yard apart for sociability.

The porters seemed to me very much done up and considering how cold it was even at 6 a.m. I was a good deal depressed by the situation. Personally I got warm easily enough; our wonderful Kami produced some sort of a hot meal and I lay comfortably in my sleeping bag. The one thing I could think of for the porters was the high altitude sleeping sacks (intended for IV and upwards), now at II which I had not ordered to come on next day with the second party of porters (two parties A & B each of 20 had been formed for these purposes and B were a day behind us). The only plan was to make an early start next morning and get to II in time to forestall the departure of B party. I remember making this resolve in the middle of the night and getting up to pull my boots inside the tent from under the door. I put them inside the outer covering of my flea bag and near the middle of my body – but of course they remained frozen hard and I had a tussle to get them on in the morning. Luckily the sun strikes our tents early – 6.30 a.m. or little later at III & I was able to get off about 7. I left directions that half the men or as many less if possible should come $\frac{1}{4}$ of the way down & meet the man coming up so as to get the most important load to III.

I guessed that B party after a cold night would not start before 9 a.m. and as I was anxious if possible to find a better way over the glacier I wasted some time in investigations and made an unsatisfactory new route, so that it was after 8.30 when I emerged from the trough; and a little further on I saw B party coming up. It was too late to turn them back. I found some of them had resolved they would not be able to get to III and go back to II the same day and consequently increased their loads with blankets etc determining to sleep at III. This was the last thing I wanted. My chief idea at the moment was to get useful work out of B party without risking their morale or condition as I saw we were risking that of A. So after dispatching a note to Noel at II I conducted B party

slowly up the glacier. After making a convenient dump and
sending down B party I got back to Camp III early
afternoon somewhat done and going very slowly from
want of food at the last. In camp nothing doing. All porters
said to be sick and none fit to carry a load. Irvine and Odell
volunteered to go down to the dump and get one or two
things specially wanted – e.g. Primus Stoves, – which was
done. The sun had left the camp some time before they
returned. A very little wall building was done this day,
notably round the N.C.O.'s tent, otherwise nothing to
improve matters. The temperature at 5 p.m. (we hadn't
thermometers the previous night) was observed to be 2° F –
30 of frost an hour before sunset –; under these conditions it
is only during the sunny, windless, hours that anything to
speak of can be done; this day there were such hours but I
gather that sahibs as well as porters were suffering from
altitude lassitude.

May 7:
The night had been very cold – $21\frac{1}{2}°$, i.e. 53° of
frost. Personally I slept beautifully warmly and yet was not
well in the morning. Odell and Irvine also seemed distinctly
unfit. I decided to send Hazard down with some of A
party to meet at the dump and bring up some of B party (it
had been arranged that some of this party should come up
again). Investigation again showed that no porters were fit
to carry loads; several were too unwell to be kept up at III.
They had to be more or less pulled from their tents: an hour
and a half must have been taken in getting their meal of

tsampa which they must clearly have before going down; and much time too in digging out the sicker men who tried to hide away in their tents – one of them who was absolutely without a spark of life to help himself had swollen feet and we had to pull on his boots without his socks; he was almost incapable of walking; I supported him with my arm for some distance and then told off a porter to do that; eventually roped in three parties in charge of the N.C.O. I sent them off by themselves from the dump – where shortly afterwards I met Hazard. Four men of B had gone on to III but not to sleep. Three others whom we now proceeded to rope up and help with their loads alone consented to stay there. A second day therefore passed with only 7 more loads got to III and nothing done to establish the camp in a more comfortable manner, unless it counted that this third night each of the six men would have a high altitude sleeping sack; and meanwhile the morale of A party had gone to blazes. It was clear to me that the morale of porters must be established if possible at once by bringing B party up and giving them a day's rest to make camp.

May 8:
I made another early start and reached Camp II at 9 a.m. – and here met Norton and Somervell. By some mental aberration I had thought they would only reach II on this day – they had proceeded according to programme and come to Camp II on the 7th. We discussed plans largely while I ate breakfast, in the mild sheltered sunny al fresco of II (by comparison). N agreed with my ideas and we

despatched all remaining B party to III with Somervell, to
pick up their loads at the dump and carry them on. A had
been filled up the previous night with hot food and were
now lying in the sun looking more like men; the only
question was whether in future to establish the correct
standard and make them carry all the way to III and back
as was always done in 1922; I was strongly opposed to this
idea, the best way of re-establishing their morale I thought
would be to give them a job well within their powers and, if
they improved as I hoped, they might well carry loads the
$3/_4$ journey to the dump on three successive days – while B
could ferry the last quarter once or twice on the two of the
days when they would not be engaged in making camp. –
This was agreed to more particularly by Geoffrey Bruce,
who really runs the porters altogether and who had now
come up from I.

A day of great relief this with the responsibility shared or
handed over; and much lying in the sun and untroubled
sleep at Camp II.

May 9:
I intended going ahead of the party to see how things were
moving at III – for this day the camp was to be made
wonderful. Seven men with special loads, fresh heroes from
the base were to go through to III; the A men to return
from the dump to II. As it turned out I escorted the first
batch who were going through to III. The conditions when
we emerged from the trough were anything but pleasant;

under a grey sky a violent wind was blowing up the snow; at moments the black dots below me on the glacier all except the nearest were completely lost to view. The men were much inclined to put down their loads before reaching the dump and a good deal of driving had to be done. Eventually after waiting some time at the dump I joined Norton and Geoff and we escorted the last three loads for III the last bit of the way. On such a day I did not expect III to be more congenial than it had been. However it was something to be greeted by the cheery noise of the Roarer Cooker; the R.C. is one of the great inventions of the Expedition; we have two in point of fact, one with a vertical, and one with a horizontal flame – a sort of super Primus stove.

Irvine and Odell had evidently been doing some useful work. It had been a triumph getting the R.C. to Camp III – it is an extravagant load weighing over 40 lbs and it now proved to be even more extravagant of fuel than had been anticipated; moreover its burning was somewhat intermittent and as the cook even after instruction was still both frightened and incompetent when this formidable stove was not functioning quite sweetly and well, a sahib had often to be called in to help. Nevertheless the R.C. succeeded in cooking food for the troops and however costly in paraffin oil that meal may have been it made the one great difference between Camp III as A party experienced it and Camp III now. Otherwise on this day, set apart for the edification and beautification of this camp,

the single thing that had been done was the erection of one
Mead tent to accommodate 2 more sahibs (only 2 more
because Hazard came down this day). And no blame to
anyone; B party was much as A party had been – in a
state of oriental inertia; it is unfair to our porters perhaps
to class them with Orientals in general but they have this
oriental quality that after a certain stage of physical
discomfort or mental depression has been reached they
simply curl up. Our porters were just curled up inside their
tents. And it must be admitted that the sahibs were most
of the time in their tents – no other place being tolerable.
Personally I felt that the task of going round tents and
seeing how the men were getting on and giving orders
about the arrangements of the camp now naturally fell to
Geoffrey Bruce whose 'pigeon' it is to deal with the
porters. And so presently in my old place, with Somervell
now as a companion instead of Hazard I made myself
comfortable; i.e. I took off my boots and knickers put on
my footless stockings knitted for me by my wife for the
last expedition and covering the whole of my legs, a pair of
grey flannel bags and two pairs of warm socks besides my
cloth-sided shoes, and certain garments too for warming
the upper parts, a comparatively simple matter. The final
resort in these conditions of course is to put one's legs into
a sleeping sack. Howard and I lay warmly enough and
presently I proposed a game of picquette and we played
cards for some time until Norton & Geoff came to pay us a
visit and discuss the situation. Someone a little later tied
back the flaps of the two tents facing each other so that

after N. & G. had retired to their tent the other four of us were inhabiting as it were one room and hopefully talked of the genius of Kami and the Roarer Cooker and supposed that a hot evening meal might sometime come our way. Meanwhile I produced 'The Spirit of Man' and began reading one thing and another – Howard reminded me that I was reproducing on the same spot a scene which had occurred two years ago when he and I lay in a tent together. We all agreed that Kubla Khan was a good sort of poem. Irvine was rather poetry shy but seemed to be favourable impressed by the Epitaph to Gray's Elegy. Odell was much inclined to be interested and liked the last lines of Prometheus Unbound. Somervell who knows quite a lot of English literature had never read a poem of Emily Brontë's and was happily introduced. ------ And suddenly hot soup arrived.

The following night was one of the most disagreeable I remember. The wind came in tremendous gusts and, in spite of precautions to keep it out the fresh snow drifted in; if one's head were not under the bedclothes one's face was cooled by the fine cold powder and in the morning I found 2 inches of snow all along my side of the tent. It was impossible to guess how much snow had fallen during the night when one first looked out. The only certain thing was the vile appearance of things at present. In a calm interval one could take stock of a camp now covered in snow – and then would come the violent wind and all would be covered in the spindrift. Presently Norton and Geoff came into our

tent for a pow-pow. G. speaking from the porters' point of
view was in favour of beating a retreat. We were all agreed
that we must not risk destroying the morale of the porters
and also that for two or three days no progress could be
made towards the North Col. But it seemed to me that in
the normal course of events the weather should now re-
establish itself and might be even sufficiently calm to get
something done that afternoon, and that for the porters the
best thing of all would be to weather the storm up at III. In
any case it would be early enough to decide for a retreat next
day. These arguments commended themselves to Norton
and so it was agreed. Meanwhile one of the most serious
features of the situation was the consumption of fuel. A box
of meta and none could say how much paraffin (not much
however) had been burnt at II; here at III no water had yet
appeared, and snow must be melted for everyone at every
meal – a box of meta had to be consumed here too, and
Primus stoves had been used before the Roarer made its
appearance yesterday. Goodness knows how much oil it has
used. It was clear that the first economy must be in the
number of sahibs (6) at III. We planned that Somervell,
Norton, and Odell should have the first whack at the
North Col, and Irvine and I finish the good work next
day – Irvine and I therefore must go down first. On the
way down Irvine suffered very much and I somewhat from
the complaint known as glacier lassitude – mysterious
complaint, but I am pretty certain in his case the sun and
the dazzling light reflected from the new snow had
something to do with the trouble.

A peaceful time at II with Beetham and Noel.

May 11:
The weather hazy and unsettled looking. I despatched 15
loads up to the dump and arranged for the evacuation of
two sick men of whom one had badly frost bitten feet
apparently, a Lepcha, unfit for this game and the other was
Sanghi, Kellas's old servant who has been attached to Noel
this expedition and last, a most valuable man, who seemed
exceedingly ill with bronchitis. The parties had been gone
half an hour before we were aroused by a shout and learned
that a porter had broken his leg on the glacier. We quickly
gathered ourselves into a competent help party and had
barely started out when a man turned up with a note from
Norton to tell me as I half expected that he had decided to
evacuate III for the present and retire all ranks to the B.C.
The wounded man turned out to be nearer at hand and not
so badly wounded (a bone broken in the region of the knee)
as I feared.

This same evening Beetham, Noel, Irvine and I were back
at the B.C. the rest coming in next day.

Well that is the bare story of the reverse, so far as it goes.
I'm convinced Norton has been perfectly right. We pushed
things far enough. Everything depends on the porters and
we must contrive to bring them to the starting point – i.e.
III at the top of their form. I expect we were working all
the time in '22 with a smaller margin than we knew – it

certainly amazed me that the whole bundobust so far as porters were concerned worked so smoothly. Anyway this time the conditions at III were much more severe and notably were temperatures lower, but the wind was more continuous and violent. I expect that these porters will do as well in the end as last time's. Personally I felt that I was going through a real hard time in a way I never did in '22. Meanwhile our retreat has meant a big waste of time. We have waited down here for the weather – at last it looks more settled and we are on the point of starting up again. But the day for the summit is put off from the 17th to the 28th and the great question is will the monsoon give time?

Base Camp
May 16, 1924

My dear Mother,

I don't know whether you will be back from Aix by now, or rather by the time this reaches you am sure you should be. I am not going to tell you all my news – I have written a huge long journal letter to Ruth which I hope you will see one way or another. The great thing is that I am very fit & happy. Norton is an ideal commander. He has put me as mountain leader entirely in charge of everything from Camp III onwards & we work out all plans together in complete harmony.

Our first journey up the glacier was naturally a trying ordeal – a question partly of trying to preserve porters from the effects of cold & altitude & partly of driving them to help themselves or to do things they didn't want to do – & porter-driving is not a sport & does not amuse me at all. I can communicate with some of the porters who understand Hindustani; but that is not like speaking their language – I can't communicate freely with them & it is an effort all the time. We had some casualties too. But on the whole we have come out of a bad time very well. The retreat was inevitable if we were to have a fair chance later on. It was a great disappointment of course & has put back the main attack 11 days – to May 28 for the final day – which brings it very late in view of the possibility of an early monsoon which seems not unlikely.

It is a very nice party. Irvine is the star of the new members. He is a very fine fellow, has been doing excellently up to date & should prove a splendid companion on the mountain. I should think the Birkenhead News, is it? ought to have something to say if he & I reach the top together. The critical day will perhaps be the one before the last, pushing up the highest camps – provided that goes well Irvine & I should have a very good chance of reaching the top. But it's a long way to go & there are many obstacles. The great thing is that we have a thorough organisation & nothing like discord this time – & for me that I'm strong & fit.

Mail has been wretched – my last letters from England were dated March 25 or thereabouts & I feel terribly out of touch. I hope the next mail will bring a letter from you. I am in communication will Mary who sends me news of the weather in Ceylon – but even her last news was nearly a month old and it is difficult to establish any definite connection between the weather here & the appearance of the monsoon current in Ceylon.

We are off up the glacier again to-morrow – Better luck this time! The old gang go first – & really except for Irvine will do all the work for the first attempt – & I can hardly believe there'll be a second (1) because we are going to succeed and (2) because there won't be time.

The weather looks more settled at last – no wind early this morning & less than likely all day. Even so I suppose we may have some cold times at III.

Nothing settled yet as you may imagine about the return journey. I still hope to be in England by early August.

Much love to you both
Your loving son,
George

After the struggles of the first two weeks of May, the climbing party tried again. This time they did make it up to the North Col (or Chang La, in Tibetan) to establish the crucial Camp IV – the launch pad for any summit assault. The new effort was again exhausting, and they had to retreat a second time to lower camps to recuperate. George wrote another long account of the push to Ruth, which she typed up and forwarded on to his mother and father.

*

Camp 1

May 27, 1924

It has been a bad time altogether. I look back on tremendous effort and exhaustion and dismal looking out of a tent door into a world of snow and vanishing hopes - - - and yet, & yet, & yet there have been a good many things to set on the other side. The party has played up wonderfully. The first visit to the North Col was a triumph for the old gang. Norton and I did the job and the cutting of course was all my part – so far as one can enjoy climbing above Camp III I enjoyed the conquest of the ice wall and crack, the crux of the route and the making steps too in the steep final 200 feet. Odell did very useful work leading the way on from the camp to the Col; I was practically bust to the world and couldn't have led that half hour though I still had enough mind to direct him. We made a very bad business of the descent. It suddenly occurred to me that we ought to see what the old way

down was like. Norton and I were ahead unroped and
Odell behind in charge of a porter who had carried up a
light load. We got only ground where a practised man can
just get along without crampon (which we hadn't with us)
chipping occasional steps in very hard snow or ice. I was all
right ahead but Norton had a nasty slip and then the
porter, whose knot didn't hold so that he went down some
way and was badly shaken. Meanwhile I below, finding the
best way down, had walked into an obvious crevasse; by
some miscalculation I had thought I had prodded the snow
with which it was choked and where I hoped we could
walk instead of cutting steps at the side of it – all the result
of mere exhaustion no doubt. – But the snow gave way and
in I went with the snow tumbling all round me, down
luckily only about 10 feet before I fetched up half blind and
breathless to find myself most precariously supported only
by my ice axe somehow caught across the crevasse and still
held in my right hand – and below was a very unpleasant
black hole. I had some nasty moments before I got
comfortably wedged and began to yell for help up through
the round hole I had come through where the blue sky
showed – this because I was afraid my operations to
extricate myself would bring down a lot more snow and
perhaps precipitate me into the bargain. However I soon
grew tired of shouting – they hadn't seen me from above –
and bringing the snow down a little at a time I made a hole
out towards the side (the crevasse ran down a slope) after
some climbing, and extricated myself – but was then on the
wrong side of the crevasse, so that eventually I had to cut

across a nasty slope of very hard ice and further down some mixed unpleasant snow before I was out of the wood. The others were down by a better line 10 minutes before me. That cutting against time at the end after such a day just about brought me to my limit.

So much for that day.

My one personal trouble has been a cough. It started a day or two before leaving B.C. but I thought nothing of it. In the high camp it has been the devil. Even after the day's exercise I have described I couldn't sleep but was distressed with bursts of coughing fit to tear one's guts – and a headache and misery altogether; besides which of course it has a very bad effect on one's going on the mountain. Somervell also has a cough which started a little later than mine, and he has not been at his physical best.

The following day when the first loads were got up to Camp II in a snow storm Somervell and Irvine must have made a very fine effort hauling loads up the chimney.

Poor old Norton was very hard hit altogether hating the thought of such a bad muddle and himself not really fit to start out next day – nor were any of us for that matter and it looked 10 to 1 against our getting up with all that snow about, let alone get a party down. I led from the camp to a point some little distance above the flat glacier – the snow wasn't so very bad as there had been

no time for it to get sticky, still that part with some small
delays took us 3 hours; then Somervell took us up to
where Geoff and Odell had dumped their loads the day
before and shortly afterwards Norton took the lead;
luckily we found the snow better as we proceeded,
Norton alone had crampons and was able to take us up to
the big crevasse without step cutting. Here was had half an
hour's halt and about 1.30 I went on again for the steep
200 ft and so the point where the big crevasse joins the
corridor. From here there were two doubtful stretches.
Norton led up the first while the two of us made good at
the corner of the crevasse – he found the snow quite good.
And Somervell led across the final slope (following
Hazard's just discernible tracks). Norton and I had an
anxious time belaying and it began to be cold too as the
sun had left us. Somervell made a very good show getting
the men off – but I won't repeat my report. Time was
pretty short as it was 4.30 when they began to come back
using Somervell's rope as a handrail. Naturally the
chimney took some time. It was just dark when we got
back to camp.

Norton has been quite right to bring us down for rest. It is
no use sending men up the mountain unfit. The physique of
the whole party has gone down sadly. The only chance
now is to get fit and go for a simpler quicker plan. The only
plum fit man is Geoffrey Bruce. Norton has made me
responsible for choosing the parties of attack, himself first
choosing me into the first party if I like. But I'm quite

doubtful if I shall be fit enough. But again I wonder if the monsoon will give us a chance. I don't want to get caught but our three day scheme from the Chang La will give the monsoon a good chance. We shall be going up again the day after tomorrow. – Six days to the top from this camp!

P.S. the parts where I boast of my part are put in to please you and are not meant for other eyes.

Camp I
May 28, 1924

My dear Mary,

Many thanks for three communications. I write in great
haste as I have had very short notice of mail going out. It is
impossible to tell you much of our plans. Everything has
been delayed again as you will have learnt before you get
this. I'm due to make the first dash with Geoffrey Bruce &
arrive at the top 7 days hence – but we may be delayed or
caught by the monsoon or anything. It will be a great
disappointment if I can't work in my visit to you, if only
for 2 or 3 days. So glad you like the hill station. It sounds
glorious.

This party has been badly knocked but we still have some
guts among us I hope.

Love to you all.
Your loving brother,
George

Camp I
May 28, 1924

My dear Mother,

Many thanks to you for three letters which have come all
in the last few days from Aix. I am so glad to think of you
enjoying that country which I have often liked on the
way through to it from Chamonix. And you've seen
Mont Blanc! that's great. It's a wonderful mountain
mass altogether & I should like to have been with you &
pointed out the various peaks & points & show you where
I had been.

Stupidly I've been caught by a short notice of the mail going
out; I have spent a lot of time trying to write a communiqué
for Norton – the one about the way up to the Chang La to
which you will have seen – & so have none left for my own
letters.

It has been a hard time altogether & depressing – but we
remain undepressed. The train is all laid now – we are
recuperating. Our plan has to be greatly modified. If I'm
fit for the job I shall go up first with Geoffrey Bruce, who
is at present the fittest of the lot – it will be a great
adventure if we get started before the monsoon hits us –
with just a bare outside chance of success & a good many
chances of a very bad time indeed. I shall take every care
I can you may be sure.

Norton, Somervell, Irvine & Geoff here with me – a good party. Oxygen is condemned in order to save porters or Irvine & I would have been together.

Much love to you both
Your loving son,
George

I may get back yet in early Aug – only missing my projected visit to Mary which will be a great disappointment.

8

AFTERMATH (1924)

George and Sandy Irvine were last seen alive by Noel Odell, on June 8th. Odell had climbed to Camp V to support their summit assault and estimated they were just 800 feet from the summit when he spotted them. Odell wrote:

At 12.50, there was a sudden clearing of the atmosphere, and the entire summit ridge and final peak of Everest were unveiled. My eyes became fixed on one tiny black spot silhouetted on a small snow-crest beneath a rock-step in the ridge; the black spot moved. Another black spot became apparent and moved up the snow to join the other on the crest. The first then approached the great rock-step and shortly emerged at the top; the second did likewise. Then the whole fascinating vision vanished, enveloped in cloud once more.

Though now very much within reach of the summit, the pair were dangerously behind schedule. George's timetable had them reaching that great rock-step – now known as the formidable Second Step – some hours earlier, as it was imperative they descended back to Camp VI and safety by nightfall.

Soon after Odell's sighting, Everest's higher reaches were hit by a violent snow squall. Odell pressed on through it with a rucksack of food in the hope of giving it to the pair on their way down. He passed through Camp VI and climbed another few hundred feet higher, regularly calling out throughout the afternoon in the hope of guiding George and Irvine back in. At 4.30pm, Odell was forced to descend or he too would be caught out on the mountain's perilous slopes in darkness. He saw no sign of the pair, even after the squall passed and the clouds cleared, exposing Everest's summit, bleak and empty.

A nervous night passed for the expedition, with all members now watching Camp VI from their various viewpoints below for a torch or candlelight – any sign that would signal the pair's return to safety. There was none. Odell launched a rescue attempt at midday on June 9th with two porters. Fighting through another bitterly cold blast, he abandoned the porters at Camp V and reached Camp VI on the morning of June 10th, almost 48 hours after George and Irvine's last sighting. The tent had not been slept in and everything was exactly how Odell had last observed it. He pushed on up the mountain for two more hours, hollering for his friends desperately. There was still no sign of George and Irvine, and there was now no chance the pair could have survived that length of time at that altitude without shelter. It had become hopeless. Odell was forced to give up. He descended back to Camp VI, and at 2.10pm laid out two sleeping bags in the shape of a T, where they would be clearly visible from the North Col, 4,000 feet below. It was the pre-arranged signal for 'No trace can be found – death'. As the horror sunk in below that George and Irvine were never coming back, Odell was ordered via another pre-arranged signal (three sleeping bags in a row) to not risk losing any more lives and abandon the search.

With the remaining climbers all now suffering from a mixture of frostbite, exhaustion and heart trouble, Everest's camps were evacuated. The distraught expedition erected a memorial cairn to their lost friends and began their return journey home.

It was several days before they reached the nearest telegraph station. Ruth received the appalling news on June 19th just after 7.30pm, via a telegram from the Mount Everest Committee. She was at home in Cambridge with the children. Britain, which had followed George and the expedition's exploits, was thrown into shock. King George V issued a formal message of regret and sympathy, and a memorial service was held for the lost pair in St Paul's Cathedral in London.

The shock and despair felt by Ruth is chronicled extraordinarily painfully in her letters to George's sister in the weeks after his death.

I could write at first & feel the sublime side now I can only be silent [. . .] it is useless to speak. It has happened and one can't get out of it. Oh Mary if only it hadn't. It's so awful that they are all coming back and George not with them. They were so nearly at the end of the danger.

She had no body to bury, and not knowing what had actually happened to him haunted her. She kept thinking it must have been a terrible mistake, perhaps he was still alive somewhere.

Ruth rented out the couple's house in Cambridge and moved back to her father's house in Godalming with their three children. She couldn't bear to be there without George. According to earlier wishes George expressed if he didn't come back from the First World War, she gave away his cherished books. His godson got a mountaineering volume, and Mary was given E.M. Forster's *A Room with a View*. The Bloomsbury novelist based his lead romantic character (George Emerson) on George.

In the months that followed, Ruth tried hard to rationalise his loss. She was convinced George had no idea his death was impending or even a possibility, as he had not written any final letter to brace her. 'I think the fact that he did not shows that he had no very special feeling of what was to happen,' she told her sister-in-law. Ruth could even understand that dying may have been a desired outcome for George, either as a necessity to achieve his dream or as an alternative to having to face a lifetime of failure. But even that was not enough for her to make up for what it would do to Clare, Berry and John – aged eight, six and three at the time. 'I can believe it may have been best for him and even for me but I cannot see that it could be for the children,' Ruth wrote. 'They will never know their loss but it is utterly irreparable.'

Ruth also told her mother-in-law about an attempt to speak to her lost husband beyond the grave, which she believed had been successful. Table turning – a supernatural seance similar to a Ouija board – was common at the time, not least among families who had lost husbands and sons in the war. Ruth's reported exchange with George, which she relays to Annie verbatim, is heartrending. In it, George also foretold the death that night of a family friend. In an earlier table turning session without Ruth but also reported by her, when asked when he died, George said 'at the top'.

Ruth was a strong Christian, but refused to wear black in mourning for George because she insisted that's not how she felt about him. She also told Mary of her wish for a reunion with George one day, when she hoped they could be happy together again.

She had to wait another 18 years. Ruth died of cancer in 1942 at the age of 50.

Westbrook
Godalming
July 5, 2024

My dear Mary,

I know I ought to have written to you sooner. But what can I say. I know you and Avie will both be very sad. It will cast a shadow over the happiest memories of your childhood & when you meet together you will be saddened. George was so much looking forward to seeing you on his way back.

Of what I feel it is useless to speak. It has happened and one can't get out of it. Even now it's very hard to realise.

Grandpapa is staying here now for a day or two. I think he & certainly Grannie are so pleased with the letters and fuss & that that really helps them a lot. I haven't seen Grannie.

I have let Herschel House for a year. I don't know if I have been wise but at first I felt the only possible thing was to get away as quickly as possible. I don't know what I shall do but I suppose eventually I shall have a house somewhere of my own.

I'm sorry this is such a rotten inadequate letter. I could write at first & feel the sublime side now I can only be silent. I have had my share of happiness there is no mistake

about that. I am sending you a long letter from George that
you will like to have. You can keep it.

Love to you & Ralph & the children

Yours
Ruth

Westbrook
Godalming
July 29, 1924

My dear Mary,

I've had your letter some time but I have only just been able to settle to answer it. I have been very busy. I had to go down to Cambridge to see to the house & papers & books.

George told me a long time ago during the war that he wanted each of his friends to have a book of his. I have been seeing to that. I have chosen a mountaineering book for David as his godson & The Room with a View for you. George liked it & had often talked of it.

I am enclosing a copy of his last letter. It is the last I now know because I have heard from Colonel Norton. I have hoped George might have written again before his last climb. I think the fact that he did not shows that he had no very special feeling of what was to happen.

Oh Mary if only it hadn't. It's so awful that they are all coming back & George not there with them. They were so nearly at the end of the danger. I do still believe that in some way we don't understand it was necessary he should pass on to the next life. I can believe it may have been best for him & even for me but I cannot see that it could be for

the children. They will never know their loss, but it is
utterly irreparable.

George & I were very very happy together but we would
I believe have been even more so as time went on. Well in a
few years we may be again.

Much love to you my dear
Ruth

Westbrook
Godalming
August 8, 1924

My dear Mary,

I know [how] hard you must find it to realise that we shall
never see George again by how hard I have found it. I
suppose I do now, but for a long time I felt as though we
might really hear it was all a mistake. Your mother & father
are very pleased by all that has been said of George, so too
am I only I knew it all before. It is dreadful being so
unhappy and not having him to help me with it.

I don't believe he had any premonition of what was to
happen. It was just an accident. That is how the world goes.
I wish we could know a little more about it and whether it
was time for him to go on to the next life and so it had to
happen somehow.

I am in trouble of John now. Something has gone wrong
with his left leg. He does not use it quite right & the knee
bends in a little when he puts weight onto it. He has been
x-rayed & that shows nothing. I have taken him to see
Geoffrey Keynes & he does not think it serious & then
we took him on to Dr Elmsley, an orthopedic specialist.
He thinks the trouble is in the hip joint & that it may be
quite slight or it might be tubercular. John is now lying up
for a fortnight & is to be inspected again on the 13th.

I think it proven not to be at all serious. But it is a worry.

I am staying with Mildred just how & have left John at
Westbrook with Violet. I have Clare & Berry with me. It's
really easier to keep him quiet without the girls there. But
I shall be very glad to get back. I don't much want to be
anywhere.

I am going to Birkenhead from the 23rd to the 30th. I am
rather dreading it but Grannie made a great point of it so
I could not get out of it. I find they will be upset if I don't
wear black clothes so I shall have to. I am not doing it
because it seems to me to express a feeling about death
which I do not feel & which I think is quite unchristian.

Love to you all
Ruth Mallory

October 26, 1924

Dear Grannie,

Some little time before I came to Birkenhead I had a letter
from Will Arnold Forster to say that he fully believed he
had been in communication with George through table
turning. It had happened this way. He did not believe in it
& had never thought about it or done it. Also he had no
sure belief in the immortality of the soul. He was visiting
some people in a cottage nearby and as he was leaving one
of them said Do you ever sit. He did not know what they
meant when he understood he agreed to try. He went to
them in the evening. After waiting ten minutes with their
fingers on the table it began to move and tap out words.
And messages came through from Mr Scott the husband
of one of the people whose hands were on the table just as
they were finishing the table moved again & spelt G.E.O.
Will said 'Is that you George' the answer was 'Yes'.

I can't give you the whole conversation but he asked George
where he had been when his soul passed to the next life. The
answer was The Top. Will asked if he has any message for
his committee. The answer was 'Organic Exhaustion'.

When I went to stay in Cornwall, Will & his wife Ka & I
tried. The table started in about ten minutes. The following
conversation ensued.

Will. Do you know who is here

G.	Ruth
R.	Do you know when I am thinking of you
G.	Yes
R.	Do you know what the children & I am doing
G.	Yes
R.	Are you as happy as you were here
G.	Yes
R.	Are you active and busy
G.	Yes
R.	Do you want to send a message to Avie
G.	No Mother
W.	What do you want to say
G.	Jeremy is coming tonight
R.	Am I to write and tell your mother this
G.	Yes
R.	I'm afraid she may not like it and be shocked
G.	Of course not
W.	Have you any messages
G.	Often sit – Geoff
W.	Geoffrey
G.	Yes
W.	Go on
G.	Ke—
R.	Keynes
G.	Yes Katherine Cox. Dear people

I don't know or mind what you think about this. You chuck it straight into the waste paper basket; but I felt I ought to send the message to you and leave you to make your own judgement.

I can only tell you this that no one had tried to make it happen & whatever force moved the silly little table was quite beyond our ordinary ken. The table could not have moved as it did move with our fingers touching it as they were touching it.

John is getting on very well. He really is running well now with his legs lifted properly. I think another month will pretty well finish him.

I have just bought a dear little pony for Clare and Berry and John. They are so delighted with it. It's only just for riding. I have not bought a cart. It's only 11 hands high & vary tame & gentle. They will be able to do everything for it themselves. The both stick on nicely. I don't let John trot yet.

My love to you & Grandpapa
Yours
Ruth

CONCLUSION:

DID HE OR DIDN'T HE?

When Edmund Hillary finally reached Mount Everest's summit with Tenzing Norgay on May 29th, 1953, his first urge was not to have his photograph taken. Instead, Hillary looked. He looked around the peak, and then down the Northeast Ridge, the Tibetan side where George would have come from instead of the southern Nepalese route that Hillary had climbed. He was searching for any suggestion that George Mallory had been there before him, but found none. If George and Sandy Irvine had made it, they left behind nothing that was still visible 29 years later.

Hillary and Tenzing's success did nothing to end the debate that has raged from the day George and Irvine disappeared. To this day, whether they had made it to the top before they died and what exactly happened to them up there on the roof of the world remains mountaineering's greatest mystery.

The last man who saw them alive, Noel Odell, was

convinced they had succeeded and then died of exposure on their descent. It wasn't just how close to the summit he'd seen them or how fast they were moving at the time. Odell said it was also because he knew George. He knew George's grit, and the power of his bloody-minded determination and knew George could not have turned back empty-handed on what was his last ever attempt on Everest. George's friends agreed, including his climbing partner of 20 years, Geoffrey Winthrop Young, who said: 'Difficult as it would have been for any mountaineer to turn back, to Mallory it would have been an impossibility.'

Much of the debate hangs around the notorious Second Step and whether George and Irvine could have climbed it. It's a fearsome 100-foot-high vertical cliff, and the last serious obstacle before Everest's summit. After it, the path to the top is clear. Climbing the Second Step, especially without any modern-day equipment, would have been a huge task for George and Irvine, who were already very tired. In 1975, a Chinese team fixed a metal ladder to the step that has been used by almost all climbers ever since.

Some expert mountaineers rate the Second Step technically too difficult for George and Irvine, and hence doubted Odell's account. He must have spotted them lower down, perhaps on the First Step, they argue. Others insist the pair could have done it, especially if a snow drift had built up against it to aid their ascent. The weather in 1924 was bad enough to have done that. The celebrated American climber Conrad Anker, who has summited Everest three times, was one of those who thought it too hard. Then – after climbing it himself in 1920s clothing to try to replicate their attempt – Anker changed his mind. It would have been feasible for the pair, he now argues. Others still, who have climbed to the exact point of Odell's sighting to evaluate it, argue he must have actually seen them even higher up the mountain, perhaps climbing the easier Third Step.

On May 1st, 1999, George's body was found. To mark the 75th anniversary of their disappearance, an expedition was mounted to discover what had happened to the pair. The climber who found George was Conrad Anker, and the body's location was a snow terrace below the Northeast Ridge at an altitude of 26,700 feet, not far from his original Camp VI. The team initially thought they'd found Sandy Irvine until they spotted two labels on the body's shirt collar. These read 'G. Mallory' and the name of an outfitter, 'W.F. Paine, 72 High Street, Godalming'.

From the position George was lying in, it was almost certainly the exact spot where he had died. He was lying face down with both arms outstretched, as if he had tried to reach out to grab onto something to try to slow his fall. His body was half frozen into the mountain scree, but well-preserved by the cold. Some of him had been pecked away by Everest's alpine choughs, but large strips of clothing remained, and the skin on his back and upper arms was largely exposed, frozen alabaster white like a statue. His right leg was broken, and his left leg was crossed over it in an attempt to protect it – suggesting he had been conscious for a while. On his forehead above his left eye was a puncture wound on his skull and dried blood. Astonished and deeply moved, Anker's team reburied George under rocks and carried out a committal ceremony.

The discovery provided a few more clues, but none of them at all conclusive. George's goggles were tucked into a pocket, suggesting he had been descending in darkness. The one thing it did disprove was half of Odell's theory, that George and Irvine had died of exposure. George had fallen, and his injuries from that fall incapacitated him and eventually killed him. A snapped rope that was still around his waist suggests it's likely he was attached to Irvine at the time of the fall.

Irvine's body remains unfound. The Vest Pocket Kodak camera that the pair were known to be climbing with was not on George's body. If Irvine's body is ever found and the camera is still with him, Kodak say the film could still be developed. That, and perhaps only that, could contain the single bit of hard proof of whether they reached the summit or not.

There is another story about the summit that was passed down through our family by George's children. A romantic one, which also offers no hard proof either way. George's eldest child Clare retold it to me when I interviewed her in northern California where she was living in 1999, before her death two years later. Clare, then aged 83, said:

My father climbed Everest with a photograph of my mother and one of her letters in his jacket pocket. They were very much in love. He told her before he set out that if he ever reached the top, he would leave the picture of her there. One of the first things I asked when I was told he had been found was what was in his pockets. The letter from my mother was still there – but her picture had gone.

So many of the questions that haunted Clare, her mother Ruth and her two siblings remain unanswered, and may always be. If George had succeeded, would he have lain dying with the intense frustration that nobody would know of his feat, or would the knowledge that he had finally done it have been enough to bring him peace in his final hours alive? Did he know that Irvine would also die without being able to tell the world? Or would George's injuries have been so severe that he lost consciousness almost immediately after protecting his broken leg?

Clare's lifelong hope was that her father had got to the top and had the joy of achieving his goal, albeit for a small while. Her fear was that he knew he was dying and that he had failed. Both, however, pale in comparison with the harder truth that she had lost him forever, a point she was also happy to impress on me: 'People have asked me my whole life whether I thought he had reached the top or not', Clare said. 'It always used to rather irritate me. I didn't care whether he reached the top or not, just that he didn't come back.'

A recurring dream stayed with Clare her for many years, sparked by the phrase that was used to explain to her what had happened to her father. She was told he was 'lost on Everest'.

I liked that [she said]. Putting it that way made me think there was a chance he could one day come back down. I dreamt that there was a train coming back with these soldiers in uniform on it. My father would get out of the train, and he had come back from Everest.

George's death sadly was not the only tragedy that the Mallory family suffered in the mountains. His younger brother Trafford rose high up the RAF's ranks to serve as General Eisenhower's air component commander for the D-Day landings. Promoted to Air Chief Marshal, he was then sent out to help lead the fight against the Japanese as Air Commander-in-Chief Southeast Asia. On the flight out, on November 14th, 1944, his plane crashed into a mountainside in the French Alps in bad weather, killing Trafford, his wife Doris and all eight aircrew. Then in 1947, Clare's husband, the American scientist Glenn Millikan, also died in a freak mountaineering accident in a gorge in Tennessee. A tumbling rock hit his head as the couple were climbing together.

The circumstances of George's death on Everest, and its rights and wrongs, will be continue to be debated by mountaineers for years to come. One thing now though seems certain to me. From his letters here, and from what Ruth as well as all of his closest friends said about him, George was never going to come down from Everest alive if he failed to reach the summit. His romanticism, his drive and his stubbornness, coupled with his constant search for purpose and meaning to his life, predestined him to either succeed in 1924 or die trying. The mountaineer Jochen Hemmleb, who coordinated the 1999 expedition that found George's body, said this of him:

> I consider Mallory the first Everest junkie. He made himself dependent on Everest, on an Everest success, and therefore dependent on a public that only under-stands success in terms of whether you reach the summit, or not.

George's death brought intense and enduring sadness for his family and friends. Yet, the single greatest irony of his whole story is that his demise was integral for his legacy. A man who failed to climb Everest three times and came back to tell the story would have earned a place in history. But a man who gave his life to that cause, the pursuit of his wildest dream, earned a greater one. Maybe that's what Ruth meant when she said George's death on Everest was the best outcome for him. In dying, he also raised the bar. His courage and sacrifice inspired others to follow him until, eventually, someone did succeed.

Humanity is a funny thing. We have a soft spot for certain types of failure, and often celebrate them more than we do successes. George takes his place alongside a series of noble failures in history: Scott of the Antarctic, Amelia Earhart, Custer's Last Stand, the Battle of Arnhem. To this day, their stories captivate the imagination. It's not their achievement we revere, it's their spirit.

After a life of searching for meaning and purpose,

George was finally able to define that spirit, and he did so a year before he died. On his return from his US lecture tour in the spring of 1923, he gave the question that bugged him wherever he went some further thought. His more sincere answer was this, and it's worth repeating in full:

People ask me, 'What is the use of climbing Mount Everest?' and my answer must at once be, 'It is of no use.' There is not the slightest prospect of any gain whatsoever. Oh, we may learn a little about the behaviour of the human body at high altitudes, and possibly medical men may turn our observation to some account for the purposes of aviation. But otherwise nothing will come of it. We shall not bring back a single bit of gold or silver, not a gem, nor any coal or iron. If you cannot understand that there is something in man which responds to the challenge of this mountain and goes out to meet it, that the struggle is the struggle of life itself upward and forever upward, then you won't see why we go. What we get from this adventure is just sheer joy. And joy is, after all, the end of life. We do not live to eat and make money. We eat and make money to be able to live. That is what life means and what life is for.

For George, it was because we're here.

ACKNOWLEDGEMENTS

I would like to thank my sister Daisy for having the original spark and for her continued wisdom, my father Bill for his tireless hours of plundering dusty old trunks with me and for giving me permission to publish George's letters, my mother Anna for her digging too, as well as putting up with my endless mess, George Mallory (Junior, GLM's grandson, who has also climbed Everest) for his advice, and all of George's other grandchildren for being so supportive over this project. It's been quite the family affair – I hope George would have liked that.

My huge thanks too to Myles Archibald, Hazel Eriksson and Mark Bolland at William Collins for their wonderful enthusiasm and professionalism throughout the process of putting this book together. Not all of George's handwriting was legible at all times (to put it mildly), but together we cracked the code. In the process, I fear they too fell in love with George and his story.

GLOSSARY

Characters

Family

Mary Brooke, née Leigh-Mallory – George's elder sister

Ralph Brooke – George's brother-in-law, Royal Artillery officer who was stationed in Colombo, Sri Lanka (then known as Ceylon) with wife Mary in 1924

'Gra' – George's grandmother Mary Jebb, Annie's mother (pronounced 'Grar')

Annie Leigh-Mallory – George's mother

Beridge 'Berry' Leigh-Mallory – George and Ruth's younger daughter

Clare Leigh-Mallory – George and Ruth's elder daughter

Doris Leigh-Mallory – Trafford's wife, killed in 1944

Reverend Herbert Leigh-Mallory – George's father, parish rector

John Leigh-Mallory – George and Ruth's son

Air Chief Marshal Sir Trafford Leigh-Mallory – George's younger brother, killed in 1944

Annie Victoria 'Avie' Leigh-Mallory – George's younger sister

Ruth Leigh-Mallory, née Turner – George's wife

Hugh Thackeray Turner – George's father-in-law, Arts and Crafts architect

Friends and colleagues

William Arnold-Forster – family friend, author and Labour Party activist, who Ruth married in 1939 after his first wife died

Rupert Brooke – friend, First World War poet, died in 1915

Reverend Dr David Cranage – Secretary of the Local Lectures Syndicate and George's boss at Cambridge in 1923/24

Duncan Grant – friend, Post-Impressionist painter, Bloomsbury group member

Robert Graves – pupil and friend, poet and novelist

Sir Frank Fletcher – Headmaster of Charterhouse School (1911–1935), mountaineer

Graham Irving – Winchester College master, mountaineer, introduced George to climbing

Geoffrey Keynes – close friend from university, mountaineer

James Strachey – friend and alleged lover, psychoanalyst, Bloomsbury group member

Lytton Strachey – friend, writer and critic, Bloomsbury group member

Geoffrey Winthrop Young – friend, climber

Everest expeditions

Bentley Beetham – 1924 expedition member,
mountaineer, ornithologist

Brigadier General Charles Bruce – head of 1922 and
1924 expeditions, Army officer

Geoffrey Bruce – 1922 and 1924 expedition member,
mountaineer, Charles Bruce's cousin

Guy Bullock – friend from Winchester, 1921 expedition
member, mountaineer, diplomat

George Finch – 1922 expedition member,
mountaineer

John de Vars Hazard – 1924 expedition member,
mountaineer

Dr Richard Hingston – 1924 expedition's doctor

Arthur Hinks – Secretary of the Mount Everest
Committee

Lt Col Charles Howard-Bury – 1921 expedition leader,
army officer, mountaineer, Member of Parliament

Andrew 'Sandy' Irvine – George's climbing partner when
he disappeared, Oxford undergraduate

Dr Alexander Kellas – 1921 expedition member, chemist,
mountaineer, died 1921 in Tibet

Dr Tom Longstaff – 1922 expedition's doctor,
mountaineer

Henry Morshead – 1921 and 1922 expedition member,
mountaineer, surveyor

John Noel – 1924 expedition member, photographer

Edward 'Teddy' Norton – 1922 expedition member, 1924
deputy head of expedition, mountaineer

Noel Odell – 1924 expedition member, mountaineer, geologist

Harold Raeburn – 1921 expedition lead climber, mountaineer

Edward Shebbeare – 1924 expedition transport officer and interpreter

Dr Howard Somervell – 1922 and 1924 expedition member, surgeon, missionary

Lt Col Edward Lisle Strutt – 1922 deputy head of expedition, mountaineer, army officer

Sir Oliver Wheeler – 1921 expedition member, mountaineer, surveyor

Sandy Wollaston – 1921 expedition's doctor, explorer

Sir Francis Younghusband – explorer and Chairman of the Mount Everest Committee

Places

Charterhouse – public school in Godalming, Surrey, where George taught

Glengorse – prep school in Sussex that George attended

Herschel House – George and Ruth's home in Cambridge during the 1924 expedition

The Holt – George and Ruth's house in Godalming

Magdalene College, Cambridge – George's college at the University of Cambridge

Mobberley, Cheshire – the village where George grew up. The Mallory family occupied its vicarage for five centuries.

St John's Vicarage, Birkenhead – the vicarage George's
father moved to in 1904

Winchester College – public school in Hampshire that
George attended

Mountaineering terms

Arête – a steep-sided mountain ridge

Bergschrund – the terminal glacial crevasse abutting a
mountain face

Col – the lowest point of a ridge that connects two
mountain peaks, a dip or a saddle

Crevasse – a deep crack or opening in a glacier

Cwm – a hollow area ringed by steep slopes, often at the
head of a valley

Glacier – a body of dense ice that slowly descends a
mountain under its own weight

Meta – metaldehyde, a fuel for a camping stove

Moraine – mounds of debris, left behind by a glacier

North Col – a saddle on the sharp-edged ridge from which
the ascent of Everest from the Tibetan side begins. First
climbed by George in 1921, the site of Camp IV

Second Step – a cliff close to Everest's summit and the
last serious obstacle before the top

INDEX OF CHARACTERS